**Books are to be returned on or before
the last date below.**

19 DEC 1997	1 9 JUN 2012	
2 NOV 1998		
26 NOV 1998		
3 0 NOV 2001	-	
2 2 SEP 2005		
2 4 FEB 2020		

LIBREX—

Wildlife

THROUGH THE YEAR

Andrew Cleave

HAMLYN

Editor: Julie West
Designers: Nick Leggett and Anita Ruddell
Picture Researcher: Claire Taylor
Production Controller: Ruth Charlton

Published in 1994 by Hamlyn Children's Books,
an imprint of Reed Children's Books, Michelin
House, 81 Fulham Road, London SW3 6RB

ISBN 0 600 57725 2

British Library Cataloguing-in-Publication Data.
A catalogue record for this book is available from
the British Library

Printed in China
Produced by Mandarin Offset Ltd.

Many of the illustrations in this book come from the following books: The Hamlyn Guide to Trees of Britain and Europe, The Mitchell
Beazley Pocket Guide to Mushrooms and Toadstools, The Hamlyn Guide to British Wild Flowers, Edible and Medicinal Plants of Britain
and Northern Europe, The Hamlyn Guide to Seashores of Britain and Europe, and the Tracker Young Nature Guides.

Contents

INTRODUCTION 4

SPRING 8
Deciduous Woodland 10
Marsh 14
Hedgerow 18
Seashore 22
Lake 26

SUMMER 30
Deciduous Woodland 32
Coniferous Woodland 36
Meadow 40
Heath and Moor 44
Seashore 48
River 54
Pond 60
Farmland 64
Park and Garden 68
Town 72

AUTUMN 78
Deciduous Woodland 80
Coniferous Woodland 84
Park and Garden 88
Town 92
The Strand Line 96

WINTER 100
Deciduous Woodland 102
Coniferous Woodland 106
Mountain 110
Estuary 114
Garden 118

Glossary 122
Acknowledgements 124

Index 125

Introduction

There is always something of interest for the keen naturalist to find in the countryside, in the garden and even in the town. Only the simplest of equipment is needed in order to study the plants and animals around us, and there is something new and different to be seen at every season of the year.

TAKING FIELD NOTES

When recording something of interest, always make a note of the date, the weather conditions and the location. A simple sketch map is sometimes helpful. Note down the type of habitat, such as coniferous woodland or garden, and then take careful notes about your sightings, with the addition of plenty of sketches. For writing your notes, a pencil is most useful, as ball-point pens won't write on wet paper. Keep your notebook in a clear plastic bag in case of really heavy rain. Always write your name and address in your notebook in case you accidentally lose it, so it can then be returned if someone finds it.

PHOTO RECORDS

One of the best ways of keeping records of your sightings is by taking photos. Make sure your camera doesn't shake while you photograph wildlife, or you will end up with a blurred picture. Cover, such as bushes, can be used to get close to your subject.

Speckled wood butter-flies fight over the best spots to sun themselves in, and a sketch with arrows shows the movements they make.

COLLECTING

It's best not to remove specimens from their natural habitat. Uprooting plants and fungi, picking flowers or catching butterflies are not necessary if careful notes are taken. Sometimes a small piece of a plant, such as a few leaves or a single flower, may be helpful for identification, and can be checked against a field guide.

EQUIPMENT

Try to get in the habit of always using plastic containers to avoid the risk of breakages. Pond-dipping and seashore studies will require nets and buckets, but many other types of wildlife studies need very little equipment. Hand lenses are very helpful, and binoculars are essential for bird-watching. A camera is not essential, but can be very helpful.

BINOCULARS

Binoculars are useful for bird-watching, and are also a great help when studying mammals. Choose a pair which are not too heavy, because you will want to carry them everywhere with you. Look for the numbers on the top which tell you how powerful they are - 7 x 35 means they magnify 7 times and the diameter of the lens is 35mm - these are probably the best size. Buy the most expensive you can afford, as they will last much longer.

5

This blackbird is feeding on the white berries of mistletoe. When it has finished feeding, it will clean its beak to remove the sticky pulp of the berry by rubbing it on bark.

SPREADING SEEDS

The observant wildlife watcher will note the many ways in which seeds are spread. Some are blown by the wind, some are carried on animal fur, and some are spread by birds. In autumn, there are many berries to tempt the birds to feed. Red is a common colour for berries, but some, like mistletoe, are white. Mistletoe is a parasite on trees, and its roots grow through the bark into the wood beneath.

A YEAR-LONG PROJECT

To photograph a tree at different seasons of the year, mark a spot with a large stone or stake, and then return to exactly the same spot each time you take another picture. Take the spring picture when the tree is in flower, and choose a sunny day for the summer picture to show the tree in full leaf. A misty day with golden sunlight will help bring out the autumn colours, and a background of snow will make a dramatic winter picture.

Taking a closer look at some trees can reveal surprising additions on the bark, in the form of fungi. Most fungi appear in autumn, but some, like the larger bracket fungi, are present all year round and have rings on them. Count the rings, and then check again after a month to see if it has grown more rings.

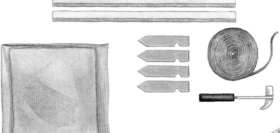

A hide provides cover for getting very close views of birds or mammals. If you sit quietly, birds will come very close without even knowing you are there.

Push the end of an empty plastic bottle through the viewing slit to get the birds used to seeing a lens.

MAKING A HIDE

Use four strong poles or stakes for the supports, a little longer than the height of the hide so they can be driven into the ground. Make the cover out of strong canvas or hessian, choosing a dull colour to blend in with trees and grass. Fix a guy rope to each pole and secure with a tent peg. Make sure that the sides do not flap in the wind, or the birds will be scared.

CODE OF CONDUCT

Always take great care not to harm the wildlife you are watching. Be careful in the breeding season when young birds or mammals are around, and be ready to move away quickly if they look distressed. If you drive the mother away, a predator may quickly move in to catch the young animal.

CONSERVATION

Pollution is a very serious threat to the countryside. Farming and industry produce poisonous wastes which may enter water supplies, and sewage from towns and cities can also cause serious pollution. Don't try to clean up pollution on your own, but join an organized group.

A large number of different trees, shrubs and wild flowers can be found in spring. The hawthorn hedge shown here can contain primrose, stitchwort and cow parsley which, together, make an eye-catching display of white and yellow. The hedge can give shelter to many creatures, like the stoat, and leaves and flowers provide food for a number of insects.

S p r i n g

Bees emerge from their nests early in the spring, and feed hungrily on the nectar from the first spring flowers.

COMING TO LIFE

Spring is an exciting time in the countryside. After the cold days and the long, dark nights of winter, the increasing strength of the sun stirs many plants and animals to activity. The warm, sunny weather encourages plants to produce new leaves and flowers, and animals to prepare for the summer breeding season. Birds sing and look for nesting sites; frogs, toads and newts arrive at ponds to lay their eggs, and bees and butterflies emerge from their winter hiding places to search for the first spring flowers from which to take a drink of nectar. Adders leave their winter dens to warm themselves on sunny banks, and lizards bask on fallen logs. Deer and foxes moult their thick winter coats and show their brighter summer coloration, and dormice, bats and hedgehogs awaken from their long winter hibernation. On the seashore, new growth appears on the seaweeds, and curious creatures like the sea lemon crawl on to rocks to lay their ribbon-like eggs.

Butterflies like the peacock come to life in spring, after a quiet winter of hibernation as adults. They are a common sight from spring onwards. Spring is also the month for courtship to take place, as each species looks for a mate. The caddis fly female searches for a mate so she can lay her eggs. These will hatch into adults the following spring.

Deciduous Woodland

Before the trees produce their summer canopy of leaves, the warm spring sunlight reaches the woodland floor and encourages many wild flowers to bloom. The trees also produce flowers, many of them in the form of catkins which produce clouds of fine pollen. Bird song fills the air, and the drumming of woodpeckers can be heard in the early mornings.

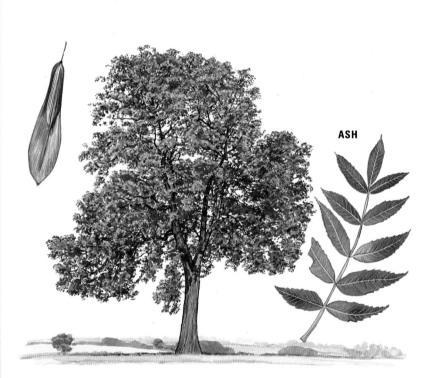

ASH

WHITE POPLAR

NEW GROWTH

Throughout the winter, most of the woodland trees will have had no leaves, but now, as the sunshine increases, their buds burst open to reveal the fresh green of the new season's growth. Often, the flowers appear before the leaves have fully opened, so that the wind can easily carry away the pollen. Many trees produce flowers in the form of delicate catkins which dangle from the tips of twigs and catch the wind. Others produce small, scented flowers which attract honey bees anxious to find food after a long winter's hibernation.

BUCKTHORN

The oak is a very long-lived tree, and even if branches have fallen off and it has become hollowed-out inside, it will still produce a few new leaves each spring. A hollow oak may also have many small creatures living inside it.

LESSER SPOTTED WOODPECKER

GREAT SPOTTED WOODPECKER

FINDING A HOME

Woodland birds must find nesting sites very quickly in the spring; they will have to compete for the best spots with the newly-arrived migrants. Birds which have found a good place for a nest advertise this by singing, so early mornings in the wood are filled with a rich chorus of bird song. Many birds have beautiful songs, but some, like the woodpeckers, drum on the trees to advertise their territories.

GREAT TIT

WOODCOCK

♀

♂

NIGHTINGALE

GOLDEN ORIOLE

TO SEED OR NOT TO SEED

Before the leaves are fully open, poplar catkins can be glimpsed on a tree. The male catkins produce a golden-yellow dust, which is the pollen, and after a few days they fall off the tree. However, the female catkins remain on the tree and, if they have received wind-borne pollen, they will develop into seeds.

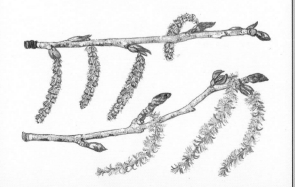

NIGHT SONGS

The nightingale sings its rich song from deep inside a bush, and is rarely seen. During the day, when other birds are singing, its song may be missed, but at night, when all others are quiet, its rich tones can be heard throughout the wood. The woodcock is also very secretive, remaining hidden during the day, but at dusk it leaves its hiding place to fly in the open around its nest site making a curious grunting sound and a shrill squeak.

GREATER STITCHWORT

The glades and clearings of deciduous woodland in spring are filled with many attractive wild flowers. They must all produce their flowers before the sunlight is blocked out by the leaves in the trees overhead.

The star-like flower clusters of wild garlic attract many insects, but the garlic-scented leaves are unpleasant to grazing animals like rabbits.

WILD GARLIC

WOOD ANEMONE

BLOSSOMING FORTH

Spring is the best time of year to look for wild flowers in a deciduous woodland. Many species produce their flowers at the same time, and some clearings are filled with a riot of colour. During the winter the plants lie dormant, with perhaps just a few leaves showing, but suddenly in spring new leaves grow and flower buds open. The flowers attract the early nectar-feeding insects like honey bees and butterflies, and once they have been pollinated they begin seed formation. Gradually the leaf canopy overhead becomes thicker, and although the sun climbs higher during the spring, the leaves block it out and the woodland floor becomes shady.

When the seeds have formed, many plants lose their leaves and start to die back, whilst others retain just a few leaves and become inconspicuous once more.

BLUEBELL

WOOD SORREL

PURPLE HAIRSTREAK

ORANGE TIP BUTTERFLY

The orange tip butterfly is one of the first to appear in the spring; the male's white wings with their large orange patches are easily spotted as it visits flowers for nectar. Females lack the orange patches, but still have the attractive mottled appearance on the underside of their wings. They lay their eggs on the cuckoo flower.

ORANGE TIP

FEEDING ON NECTAR

Sunny days in spring are ideal for watching woodland insects, especially in places where there are many wild flowers. Bees will be busy searching for nectar in order to build up their reserves in the hive after a long winter. Many spring flowers are brightly coloured in order to attract them, and some also have a strong scent. The bees collect nectar from the flowers, but they also take the golden pollen back to their hives in special 'pollen baskets' on their legs. Some flowers only give up their nectar to butterflies which have tongues long enough to reach down inside the flower. Primroses produce their nectar at the base of a tube which is too long for bees to reach, but ideal for butterflies like the brightly-coloured brimstone. Some butterflies take possession of a patch of flowers and try to keep all intruders away.

RED UNDERWING

Spring is a time for caterpillars to emerge, and feed on the food plants around them, on which the eggs were laid. The purple hairstreak prefers oak trees, brimstones prefer alder buckthorn, and red underwings are attracted to poplars.

BRIMSTONE

Marsh

After the floods and freezing weather of winter, marshes come to life in the spring. Plants which have remained hidden for most of the winter send up new leaves, or emerge from the mud below the water. After lying dormant for several months, insects are stimulated by the warmth to leave their hiding places and resume normal life once more.

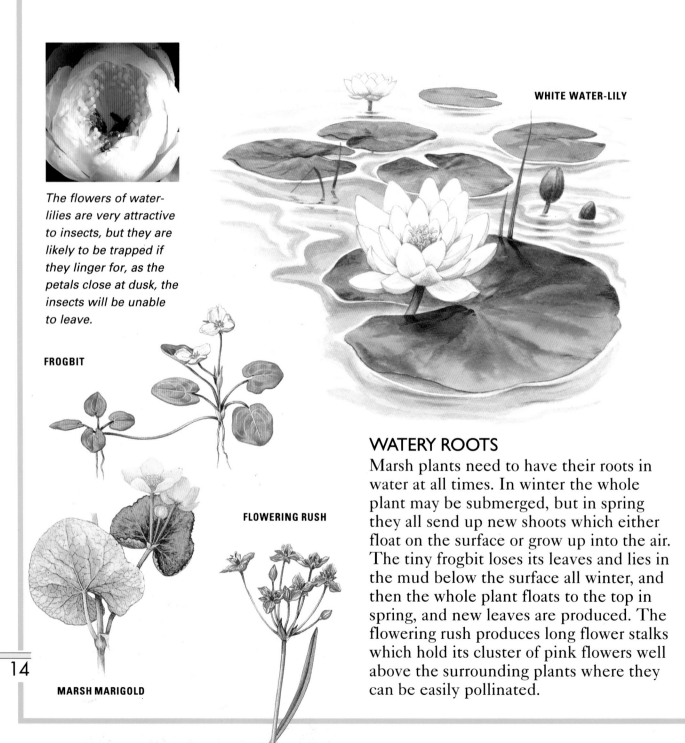

The flowers of water-lilies are very attractive to insects, but they are likely to be trapped if they linger for, as the petals close at dusk, the insects will be unable to leave.

WHITE WATER-LILY

FROGBIT

FLOWERING RUSH

MARSH MARIGOLD

WATERY ROOTS

Marsh plants need to have their roots in water at all times. In winter the whole plant may be submerged, but in spring they all send up new shoots which either float on the surface or grow up into the air. The tiny frogbit loses its leaves and lies in the mud below the surface all winter, and then the whole plant floats to the top in spring, and new leaves are produced. The flowering rush produces long flower stalks which hold its cluster of pink flowers well above the surrounding plants where they can be easily pollinated.

14

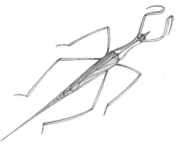

WATER STICK INSECT

Looking just like a piece of plant stem, the water stick insect lies in wait for its prey with its powerful front legs poised ready to strike if something comes close enough.

Many insects of marshes are hard to see as they blend in so well with their surroundings, but some are amongst the most colourful of all insects; the magnificent swallowtail butterfly is one of the largest and most colourful of all butterflies. Its brightly-coloured caterpillar is equally attractive.

SURVIVAL!

Many marsh insects die in the autumn, having laid their eggs in the mud or on water plants. During the winter it is only the eggs which survive, as there would be no food for the adults. These hatch in the spring, but not into the adult form of the insects; butterfly eggs will produce caterpillars, while the eggs of underwater species like the water stick insect will produce tiny nymphs which grow in stages until they reach adult size.

SWALLOWTAIL BUTTERFLY

The swallowtail's egg is laid on its foodplant, milk parsley, and the caterpillar hatches after 10-12 days.

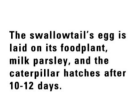

The pupa is safely attached to a plant stem by a silken thread.

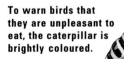

To warn birds that they are unpleasant to eat, the caterpillar is brightly coloured.

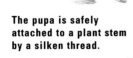

BUTTERFLY EGGS

Butterfly eggs are very small, and usually concealed in a place where predators cannot find them and where they are protected from harsh weather. They often have beautifully-sculpted shells and can be quite colourful. Some species lay their eggs in clusters, while others lay them singly. Some hatch after only a few days, while others survive all winter before hatching.

SKILLED NEST-BUILDER

Sedge warblers are skilled at building their cup-shaped nests of fine grass amongst the waving stems of reeds. Males sing from within the reeds and, although they are difficult to see, their repetitive, scratchy song can be heard from a distance. These small, drab-coloured birds are common in dense reed beds and can easily perch on the thin stems of the reeds where they search for their insect food.

SEDGE WARBLER

CETTI'S WARBLER

CANADA GOOSE

AT HOME IN WATER

Marshland birds have many ways of coping with their watery environment. Some, like the redshank and snipe, have long legs and beaks for wading and feeding in shallow water and mud, whilst others, like the Canada goose, have webbed feet for paddling, and are able to swim in deeper water. The warblers are adapted for life in waterside vegetation, being able to conceal themselves in reedbeds and perch on the thin reed stems. The Cetti's warbler is a small bird with a very loud chirruping song which it delivers from a perch, usually a bush, at the edge of the reeds. Like the other warblers, its colouring makes it difficult to see.

REDSHANK

The snipe's extremely long bill enables it to probe down into soft mud in search of worms and insect larvae. The tip of the bill is very sensitive, so the snipe can detect its prey even when it cannot see it.

THE ELEGANT GREENSHANK

The greenshank is a slim and elegant wader with grey-green legs and a long, slightly up-tilted bill. It is a lively bird, often dashing around in shallow water trying to catch small fish. Sometimes in its excitement it goes in too deep, and has to swim. Its head moves from side to side as it chases small fish through the shallows and every few seconds it will make a stab with its bill. When it does catch a fish it tips its beak back to swallow. Greenshanks also feed on worms and shrimps caught in shallow water or mud; seen from a distance when feeding it appears to be leaning forwards with its head down and tail up.

GREENSHANK

PUSSY WILLOW

DOWNY BIRCH

SWAMP CYPRESS

MARSH TREES

Trees which grow near marshes must be able to grow well in a waterlogged soil, and sometimes cope with having water swirling around the trunk. Trees in the willow family are common on marshes and grow easily in damp ground. The swamp cypress grows best in marshes and is unhappy in dry conditions, whilst others, like the downy birch and aspen, can tolerate quite damp conditions and are often found in marshes which are drying up and turning into woodland.

ASPEN

17

Hedgerow

The hedgerow is home to many plants and a great variety of birds, mammals, insects and other animals. It offers them plenty of secure hiding places, and allows small creatures to move safely through the countryside without being seen. In cold or stormy weather the hedgerow provides shelter, and on hot, sunny days it gives welcome shade.

STOAT

Each mole will make its own set of tunnels and mole hills, and if one mole meets another they fight! Breeding hills are very large and contain a nest of leaves and grasses. Moles are born naked, but fur will grow after two weeks or so.

MOLE

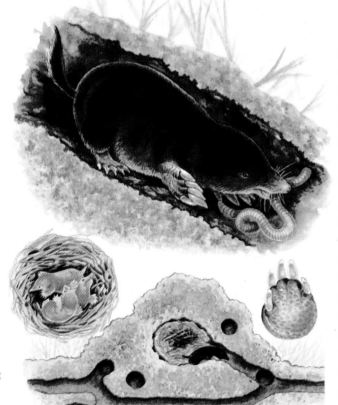

Scaling walls in pursuit of prey is very easy for young stoats, and they are always curious to see what they will find on the other side.

NESTING ACTIVITY IN SPRING

Moles and stoats are both common mammals although they are rarely seen, as moles live underground and stoats are very secretive. Both moles and stoats make nests in spring in which to give birth to their young. Moles usually have two or three young, and the stoat will have about six. They will stay with their mother until they have learnt to feed themselves. For stoats, this means learning to hunt small mammals, whilst moles must learn to find worms and other creatures in the soil.

18

GOLDFINCH

SPRING SONG

A welcome sound in the spring is the call of the cuckoo. This familiar bird is more often heard than seen, and only the male makes the well-known call. Male warblers sing from a song post near a nest site to attract a mate and warn off other males, while partridges make their calls from ground level early in the morning and late in the day.

HAZEL

A SAFE HAVEN FOR WILDLIFE

One of the commonest trees in hedgerows and some woodlands is the hazel. It is also one of the most useful for wildlife because its flowers, leaves and fruits are a good source of food. Its many branching stems provide safe nesting sites for birds, and allow small mammals like dormice to run through the hedge without touching the ground. Wild crab apple trees are covered with a mass of blossom in spring; sometimes the flowers are so dense that the leaves can hardly be seen. This blossom attracts many honey bees, and the trees buzz with activity on a sunny day.

♀

♂

GREY PARTRIDGE

RED-LEGGED PARTRIDGE

CUCKOO

WILD CRAB APPLE

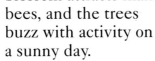

19

These five types of flower can all be commonly found in the hedgerow. Look out for their bright, attractive flowers between March and May.

PRIMROSE

FLOWERS
Early in the year, before the trees have a complete canopy of leaves, plenty of warm sunlight reaches the woodland floor and encourages a carpet of beautiful spring flowers to grow. If it is dark, few flowers will grow.

WOOLLY APHID

FLOWERS AND INSECTS
The first spring flowers are beautiful to look at, especially after a long winter, but they are also very important to insects. Many spring flowers provide valuable nectar which bees and butterflies need for energy. Some insects visit the flowers to lay their eggs. Several species of caterpillar feed on violets, eating the leaves rather than the nectar and pollen. However, some flowers, such as dog's mercury, are poisonous.

COW PARSLEY

DOG'S MERCURY

COMMON DOG VIOLET

BUGLE

CUTTING BACK
Coppicing is the traditional practice of cutting shrubs like hazel back to ground level so that the stumps sprout and produce lots of new even-sized poles. Look for coppiced areas by checking for sprouting stumps. These areas are excellent sites for butterflies and spring flowers.

SUNSHINE LOVERS

The scotch argus butterfly hibernates through the winter as a young larva, and emerges in the spring to feed, mainly on grass leaves. It loves bright days with lots of sunshine. The butterflies only live for about three weeks, but their caterpillars live for as long as ten to twelve months. The red and black leafhopper is a tiny animal, about 11mm long, which feeds on plant sap. If it is disturbed, the leafhopper will hop about from leaf to leaf. You have to be very quick to see one!

ATTACK!

Watch a shieldbug feed in hedgerow vegetation. Sometimes shieldbugs are not content to feed on plant sap, berries and fruit. Soft-bodied insects, especially if they cannot defend themselves, are a good meal. Caterpillars are very vulnerable to attack.

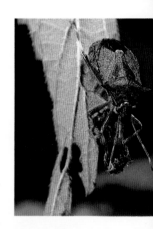

The moth and butterfly on this page both have orange and brown colours on their wings. This helps them hide themselves in the twigs and grass around them, and makes their lives much safer.

SCOTCH ARGUS

HAWTHORN SHIELDBUG

Lappet moth eggs are laid in small groups under apple and hawthorn leaves. The caterpillars vary from grey to reddish-brown.

LAPPET MOTH

RED AND BLACK LEAFHOPPER

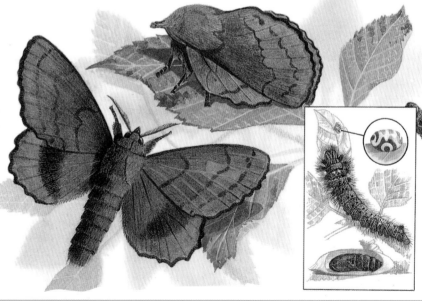

Seashore

After a winter of heavy seas and rough weather, the calmer, warm days of spring encourage many marine creatures to leave their deep water hiding places and move up on to the shore to breed. Seaweeds begin to grow again, and above the tide line the first spring flowers start to bloom.

TOUGH SURVIVORS

Seashore plants must be tough in order to withstand rough weather and tolerate the salt spray driven on to them by winter storms. They often have small waxy leaves, and flexible stems. Once the better weather of spring arrives, they are able to produce new leaves and shoots, and begin to flower. Sea buckthorn is one of the few shrubs which live really close to the sea on habitats like sand dunes; it produces many tiny flowers amongst its slender leaves; these will later develop into bright orange berries. Low growing plants like sea campion and scurvy grass are now able to send up flowering shoots in the hope of attracting pollinating insects.

Sea campion is a common plant of seashores. Its cushion of grey-green leaves supports short nodding flower stalks, and the cup-shaped white flowers are attractive to insects.

SEA CAMPION

SEA BUCKTHORN

COMMON SCURVY-GRASS

Scurvy grass has shiny green leaves on short stalks, and clusters of four-petalled white flowers. It was once used as a source of Vitamin C.

CLOUDED YELLOW BUTTERFLY

The death's head hawk moth has a striking pattern of a skull on its thorax, and its body and hind-wings are also boldly marked.

DEATH'S HEAD HAWK MOTH

Many butterflies and moths which live in warm climates are able to breed in the north during the summer, so they use southerly winds to carry them across the sea; they are frequently found near the shore after these journeys.

RESIDENTS AND MIGRANTS

The seashore is not a very hospitable place for insects, but in sunny weather some may be seen visiting flowering plants. Butterflies and moths found near the shore may be migrants which have just made a long sea crossing and are looking for flowers to give them much-needed energy. Others, like beetles, may be resident insects which have spent part of their life-cycle in a more sheltered place, and have just emerged from a long winter's hibernation as a pupa.

SILVER-Y

CUCKOO FLOWER

The oil beetle lacks true wings, and has a large shiny abdomen. Females lay many eggs which hatch into tiny larvae; these wait on flowers for a visiting bee to carry them to its nest, where they feed on honey.

OIL BEETLE

23

SEA LEMON

Sea lemons are sea slugs which live in deep water in winter, coming on to the shore in spring to feed on breadcrumb sponge, and lay their white ribbons of eggs on seaweeds. Once they have laid their eggs, they die.

SHELLS

Large numbers of empty shells can be found washed up on some seashores, especially after storms. Living molluscs should be searched for at low tide in calmer weather. Whelks and mussels live on rocky shores, especially those in exposed places, and can be very common below the high tide line. Cockles and razor shells are harder to find, as they live buried in sand, and only have a small part of the shell showing.

OYSTERCATCHER

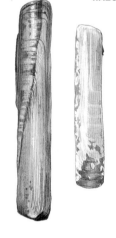

GROOVED RAZOR SHELL

COMMON WHELK

POD RAZOR SHELL

PREDATORS

Dog whelks prey on mussels and barnacles and can be seen scattered amongst their prey. Mussels are unable to escape from danger; their only defence is to close their shells tightly if they are aware of a predator. Whelks and sting winkles can drill small round holes through the shell and suck out the contents, whilst oystercatchers can use their tough beaks to hammer the shell open.

COMMON COCKLE

STING WINKLE

COMMON MUSSEL

Cockles spend most of their lives buried in sand with part of the shell showing. A live cockle's shell gapes open slightly, but if disturbed it shuts quickly with a squirt of water, and cannot easily be opened again.

THICK-LIPPED DOG WHELK

BIRDS OF THE SEASHORE

There is plenty of food on the seashore for birds. Many of them have long legs for wading in shallow water where they find their prey, and bills especially adapted to catch tiny marine organisms. Gulls are common on the shore and take a variety of foods; their noisy calls are often heard as they feed in flocks. The piping calls of wading birds are heard as they feed and display over their breeding territories.

BLACK-HEADED GULL

RINGED PLOVER

PERFECT CAMOUFLAGE

The black and white head markings of the ringed plover make it very hard to see as it sits motionless on its nest, or roosts quietly on the shore. Only when it flies does it reveal its presence.

DOG WHELKS

Most dog whelks have an off-white shell, but some show a pattern of darker stripes, thought to be the result of feeding on dark-shelled prey, like mussels. In sheltered places the shell is ridged and pointed, but in rough sites it is smoother and has a larger opening for the foot to improve its grip in stormy weather. Females lay eggs in tiny capsules attached to rocks.

DOG WHELK

25

Lake

In the depths of a large lake, the water will be cold throughout the year, but around the margins the shallow water will soon warm up in spring, and plants will start to grow. Birds and mammals become more secretive as they look for safe nesting sites, but some engage in attractive courtship displays.

LAKE MARGIN PLANTS

A very common and important plant of lake margins is the common reed; it provides safe feeding and nesting sites for many birds and has been used as a thatching material by people living near lakes for hundreds of years. Its purple flower heads start to grow in late spring.

COMMON REED

Flote grass is very tasty to grazing animals, so in order to avoid being eaten, its leaves float on the surface while its roots grow in the lake bed.

FLOTE GRASS

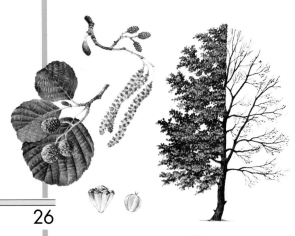

ALDER BUCKTHORN

ALDER

LAKESIDE TREES

Trees which grow beside lakes can tolerate water around their roots. The alder has a strong ridged bark and rounded leaves, and in spring produces attractive purple catkins which open to release golden pollen. If felled, the timber has a rich red colour and strong water-resistant properties; the wood is used to make clogs. The alder buckthorn is a smaller, more slender tree with white flowers in spring; it is the favourite food plant of the brimstone butterfly.

Water shrews are very good swimmers, and can often be seen in lakes and ponds in the spring. Look for the black upper part of the shrew, and white or yellow underneath.

COURTSHIP

Water birds are secretive when nesting, but their courtship displays are often very exciting. Swans ruffle their wing feathers over their backs, mallards bob their heads repeatedly, and great crested grebes stand high in the water and present each other with pondweed!

MUTE SWAN

The female mallard lays her eggs in a nest concealed in thick vegetation or a hollow tree, but once they have hatched, the tiny ducklings are taken away to feed in the margins of the lake.

MALLARD

GREAT CRESTED GREBE

BEAVERS - YOUNG AND OLD

After a long winter spent hiding in their lodge with only occasional trips outside, the fresh plant growth of spring encourages beavers to spend more and more time in the open searching for fresh food and repairing their dams. Inside the lodge, tiny young will be born, and these will at first be fed on their mother's milk, but eventually they will be given small scraps of leaves and then be coaxed into the water for their first swim.

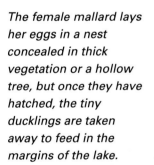

WATER SHREW

The beaver lodge is one of the largest homes made by any animal, containing huge quantities of branches and mud. In spring it will need repairs, and much time is spent finding new material on the banks of the lake.

BEAVER

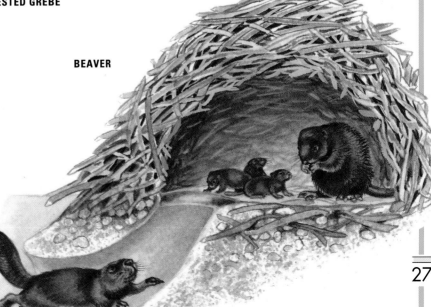

THE LIFE OF THE CADDIS

Most insect-feeding birds leave a lake in winter because insects are very hard to find. In spring, many insect nymphs and larvae which have been concealed on the bed of the lake for several months emerge from the water to complete their life-cycles as adults in the air above. The stems of emergent plants will have many empty skins of the nymphs clinging to them while the adult insects are on the wing over the water. Caddis flies are very common in freshwater, and their larvae live in protective cases made of pieces of plant stem, tiny fragments of gravel or small shells. The adult caddis flies look like slender moths with large antennae; during the day they conceal themselves on vegetation and at night they fly to find new sites to lay their eggs. The adult flies are an important source of food for birds and bats, and the larvae are preyed on by fish, newts and beetle larvae.

Female caddis flies lay their eggs on plant stems in a mass of jelly. When the larvae hatch, they build themselves a protective case.

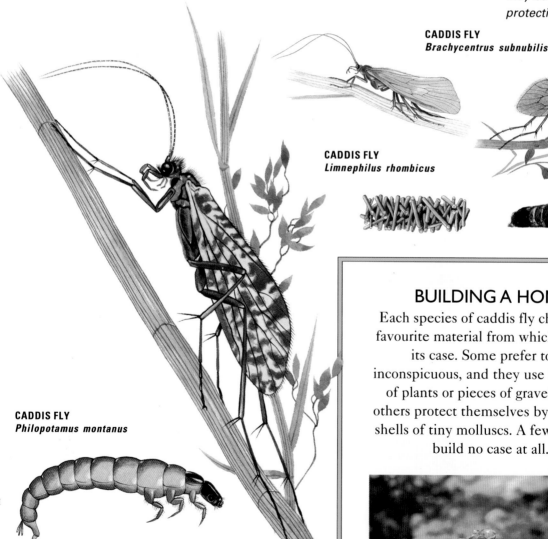

CADDIS FLY
Brachycentrus subnubilis

CADDIS FLY
Limnephilus rhombicus

CADDIS FLY
Philopotamus montanus

BUILDING A HOME

Each species of caddis fly chooses its favourite material from which to build its case. Some prefer to be inconspicuous, and they use fragments of plants or pieces of gravel, whilst others protect themselves by using the shells of tiny molluscs. A few caddises build no case at all.

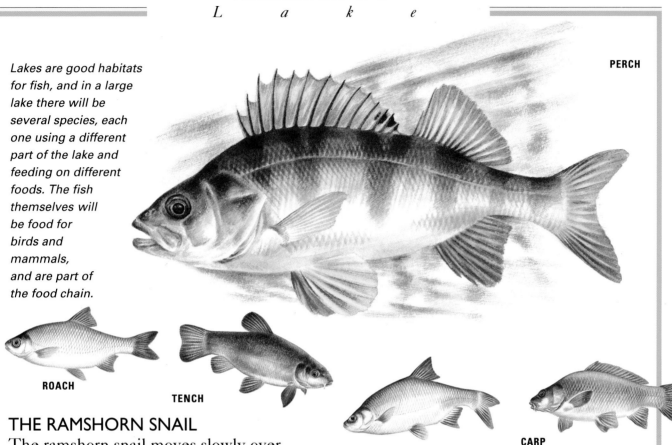

PERCH

Lakes are good habitats for fish, and in a large lake there will be several species, each one using a different part of the lake and feeding on different foods. The fish themselves will be food for birds and mammals, and are part of the food chain.

ROACH

TENCH

RUDD

CARP

THE RAMSHORN SNAIL

The ramshorn snail moves slowly over plant stems at the margins of the lake, feeding on algae and other small plants. Its tough shell protects it from all but the largest fish. It moves so slowly that algae grow on its shell, giving it a strange hairy appearance. The ramshorn lays its eggs in sausage-shaped masses of jelly stuck to plant stems; these hatch into tiny snails which must feed and grow quickly before being eaten by fish. The tiny snails are a favourite food of many lake-dwelling creatures.

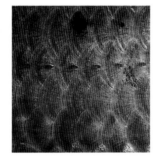

Most fish have a protective body covering of scales which overlap and give a smooth shape to the body. The scales are often coloured or patterned, and help to camouflage the fish.

THE SLIPPERY EEL

The eel is a curious snake-like fish which lacks scales; its skin is covered with a protective slime instead. It spends much of its time buried in the mud on the bed of the lake, emerging at night to feed on snails, worms, fish and anything else it can catch. When they reach full size, eels leave the lake and travel to a river to start their migration to the sea.

COMMON EEL

RAMSHORN

The seashore is home to many creatures in the summer. Some are visitors, like the common seal which hauls out on the beach to rest, but others, like the heart urchin, live there all the time, buried in the sand and out of sight. A deserted sandy beach is a safe nesting place for terns whose eggs are hard to spot amongst the shingle.

Summer

The hermit crab's soft body is protected inside the abandoned shell of a whelk. Its head and legs stick out, and it is able to scuttle around.

SUMMER FUN
A visit to the coast in summer can be very rewarding. Many birds which spend most of their lives far out to sea come to the coast to breed and can be seen at their nesting sites on land. Puffins lay their single egg at the end of a burrow deep in the cliff, and razorbills nest in rock crevices, but both birds can be watched as they sit on rock ledges, sometimes forming colonies of thousands. Terns nest on beaches, concealing their eggs by means of excellent camouflage. Herring gulls patrol the breeding colonies of other seabirds looking for unguarded eggs or chicks which they can eat. Rock doves are the ancestors of town pigeons; their nests are built on ledges and in caves, and they feed along the cliff tops. The cliffs and beaches become colourful with wild flowers in summer; thrift and rock sea spurrey form pink carpets on some cliffs and on sand dunes prickly clumps of sea holly grow among the marram grass.

Rock pools form when the tide goes out, leaving water trapped amongst the rocks. Small sea creatures which must remain underwater can live there until the tide returns. Beadlet anemones extend their tentacles into the water to catch lots of tiny fish and shrimps; when danger threatens them, they close up and look like a blob of jelly.

Deciduous Woodland

In mid-summer, a woodland is filled with scents, sounds and colours. The spring bird-song is replaced by the buzz of bees and hoverflies, and beneath the ever-thickening canopy of leaves, woodland flowers open and attract butterflies which flit through sunny glades.

WIDESPREAD SYCAMORE

The fresh green leaves of sycamore, seen first in spring, become dull and thick in mid-summer, and the spreading crown of the tree blocks the light to the woodland floor below. After pollination, the flowers begin to turn into the winged 'helicopter' seeds which spread everywhere, making this a very common tree.

SYCAMORE

WILD BLACKBERRY

WILD RASPBERRY

FRUITS OF THE FOREST

Many woodland flowers and shrubs produce berries which can be eaten, and in mid-summer, when they are in full bloom, they attract a variety of insects to pollinate them so that they can set seed and produce their fruits. Wild blackberries are very common flowering shrubs, attracting many bees, butterflies, hoverflies and other insects. They sometimes form huge patches in woodland clearings. Wild raspberries are harder to find, and need plenty of sunshine before their fruits will ripen.

WILD STRAWBERRY

Wild strawberries like sunny banks and wood-land paths where they can catch the sun. You can recognize the wild strawberry by its white flowers and small, but delicious, red berries.

FOXGLOVE

FLOWER-FILLED GLADES

Sunny glades are the best places to look for flowers such as the foxglove with its tall spikes of purple-pink flowers. The dog rose scrambles over other shrubs on the edges of the wood, producing its delicately-scented pink or white flowers which are favourites of hoverflies. The bright flowers of yellow archangel grow in spikes.

HOVERFLY

The purple emperor is a large butterfly. Males have a beautiful purple sheen on their wings, and they show this off by sitting in sunny places gently opening and closing them.

PURPLE EMPEROR

DOG ROSE

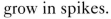

STRANGELY ATTRACTIVE

Lords and ladies, found in slightly shaded places, has large pointed leaves, sometimes with spots, and flowers which have a green hood with a yellow or purple spike inside it. Flies are attracted to its strange smell, and are trapped inside the base of the flower, only to be released when they are covered with pollen.

SPECKLED WOOD

YELLOW ARCHANGEL

LORDS AND LADIES

FIGHTING WOODS

Male speckled wood butterflies fight over the best sunny places, and will drive away rivals who enter their territories, so they are often seen engaged in fluttering fights. The loser will fly back to his own territory and the winner will give a display flight to show that he has won.

NUTHATCH

REDSTART

PIED FLYCATCHER

SEARCHING FOR FOOD

The redstart is an attractive migrant bird which spends its winters in Africa, but spends the summer in the woods of Europe. It often perches in a secret place in a leafy tree, and flies out into the open to catch a fly, or land on the ground to pick up an insect. The song, a loud whistle followed by shorter ticking sounds, gives away the hiding place; when in view redstarts are seen to quiver their tails up and down. The nuthatch nests in hollow trees, and is a very agile mover, being able to move upwards or downwards on the tree trunk in its search for insects.

Pied flycatchers are summer visitors which nest in old woodlands. The boldly-marked male is hard to see in the dappled light of a wood when it is perching high up in the leaf canopy.

Fox cubs come out of their underground earth to play in summer and learn about their surroundings. At first, their mother brings them food, but they must learn how to find their own as the end of summer approaches.

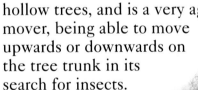

RED FOX

CREATURES OF THE NIGHT

Wood mice remain hidden during the day, but come out at night to look for food on the woodland floor. In summer, they make leafy nests in holes in the ground or hollow trees, and produce litters of about six young. There is plenty for them to eat in a wood as they are fond of flowers, seeds, fruits, shoots and even insects. Mice spend a lot of time grooming themselves to keep clean and free from parasites. Bats are also active at night, flying through the dark to find insects to eat. They will breed in mid-summer, and are a very common sight until winter, when they will find a cold, dark place to hibernate.

WOOD MOUSE

If one mouse invades the territory of another mouse, there will be a fight until one of the mice gives in and leaves. The noisy squabbling attracts predators like foxes and weasels, and both mice may end up being caught and eaten!

LEISLER'S BAT

SEROTINE BAT

In summer, badgers can find plenty of food in the woods, especially if the weather is damp. They are fond of earthworms and slugs, but will eat almost anything they find, including fruits and berries. As they search for grubs, they make scratch marks in the woodland floor.

BADGER

BADGER WATCHING

Summer evenings are the best times to watch badgers at their setts. It is important not to get too close, or to let any human scent drift towards the sett. They usually emerge at sunset, while there is still some light, and spend some time grooming near the entrance before moving off to look for food.

Coniferous Woodland

Insects are very busy in coniferous woods in summer. Ants keep the woodland floor clear of dead remains, sawfly and moth larvae nibble the pine needles, and birds make meals of the insects. Cones begin to form on the trees, and juniper develops its sweet-smelling fruits.

Wood ants are important insects in coniferous woods, and form very large colonies. The workers scour the woodland floor looking for waste matter, dead and living insects, or other food material which they take back to the nest. Others collect fallen pine needles to help build and repair the nest.

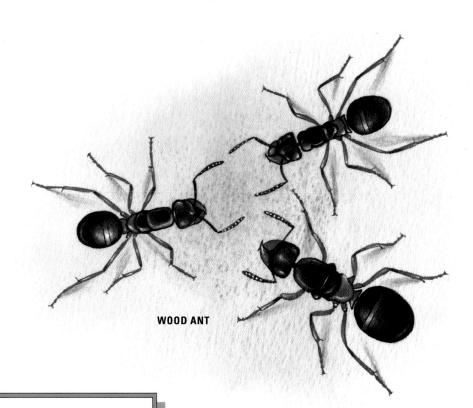

WOOD ANT

HUNGRY LARVAE

Sawflies are related to bees, wasps and ants, and their leaf-eating larvae look like caterpillars, but they have six or more pairs of false legs at the back, instead of the five which caterpillars have. These pine sawfly larvae are feeding on pine leaves. Adult sawflies have two pairs of wings, but they are poor fliers.

PINE SAWFLY

WOOD WHITE BUTTERFLY

Wood white butterflies are usually only found where vetch occurs in coniferous woods, so they are rather scarce. They are poor fliers, so will often only be found in a limited area. These butterflies are beautiful and delicate, and have tiny wings.

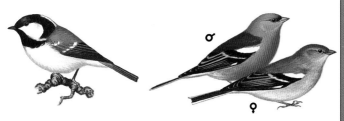

COAL TIT **CHAFFINCH**

THE INSECT EATERS

The agile coal tit finds plenty of insect food amongst pine needles in summer, and feeds its young on a diet of sawfly larvae and other insects. Chaffinches are mostly seed eaters, but in early summer seeds are hard to find, so they will be forced to eat some insects as well.

AROMATIC 'BERRIES'

The green 'berries' of juniper are really fleshy cones with a strong scent. Birds such as thrushes will eat them, and they can also be used to flavour cooking, and the alcoholic drink of gin.

SITKA SPRUCE

COMMON JUNIPER

COMMON LARCH

CONIFERS

The larch is an unusual conifer which drops its needles in winter. In summer the soft needles are a bright clear green, but they turn golden brown before falling in autumn. Larches have attractive red female flowers along the spindly twigs, and these develop into small, lightweight cones. The sitka spruce is a much hardier evergreen tree with tough spiky needles and thicker cones which hang downwards.

37

The broad buckler fern has scales on its leaf stalks with a dark line in the middle, and it is one of the few ferns which keeps green leaves in the winter. It usually grows in thick clumps in shady places.

BROAD BUCKLER FERN

WHITE, BLUE AND YELLOW

Wood sage has leaves which look like the garden herb, sage, but it has a different scent and is not used in cooking. Its spike of creamy-white flowers is attractive to small bees. Heath speedwell grows in creeping clumps near paths and in open places, producing upright spikes of blue flowers. The bright yellow flowers of tormentil are easy to spot, but when the plant is not flowering, its trailing stems are easily overlooked.

Bilberry forms shrubby clumps on the woodland floor, producing small clusters of red flowers which are followed by edible purple-black berries in late summer.

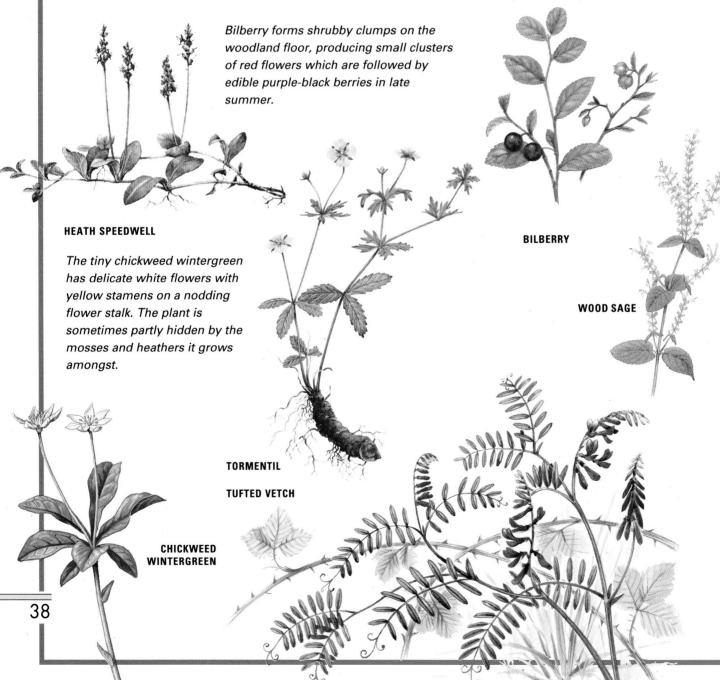

HEATH SPEEDWELL

The tiny chickweed wintergreen has delicate white flowers with yellow stamens on a nodding flower stalk. The plant is sometimes partly hidden by the mosses and heathers it grows amongst.

BILBERRY

WOOD SAGE

TORMENTIL

TUFTED VETCH

CHICKWEED WINTERGREEN

IS A POLECAT A CAT?

No. Polecats are ferret-like creatures which eat small birds and mammals which they capture with their sharp teeth. They usually hunt on the ground and take food to a well-hidden den. They have a strong musky scent which they use to mark their territories.

POLECAT

FALLOW DEER

Fallow deer are very variable in colour, mostly being brown with dappled markings, but also ranging from black to white. The summer coat is more boldly marked than the winter coat. During the summer, males grow their new set of antlers; at first the small antlers are covered with skin called 'velvet', but when they have finished growing, the skin dies and is rubbed off on branches. Older deer have larger antlers which they use for fighting with other males in the autumn.

RECORDING A TRACK

Plaster casts make good records of the mammals you have been studying, and do no harm to the environment. Place a ring of cardboard around the track, mix plaster of Paris with clean water and, when you have a smooth paste, pour it into the mould. Leave it to set for about 25 minutes then carefully lift it up.

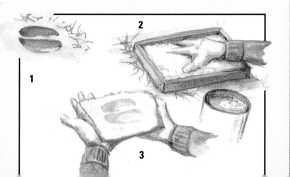

HIDDEN FAWNS

The newly-born fawn is left by its mother in a safe hiding place while she goes off to browse on bushes nearby. Its dappled coat helps it to blend in with the leaves on the woodland floor. When it can walk well, it follows her around.

39

Meadow

A flower-filled meadow is a colourful place in mid-summer; orchids, buttercups, cranesbills and the grasses themselves make a bright and multi-coloured patchwork. Butterflies love meadows, and many birds are able to find food and safe nesting sites amongst the grasses. Flower-filled meadows are becoming scarce as more and more pesticides are used by farmers.

GREATER BUTTERFLY ORCHID

BEE ORCHID

PYRAMIDAL ORCHID

EARLY PURPLE ORCHID

COLOURFUL ORCHIDS

Orchids grow well in meadows which are free from pesticides and ploughing, and are sometimes quite common. Their leaves are distasteful to grazing animals, so they are usually left alone, and their flower spikes are able to grow above the other plants and attract pollinating insects like bees. Each orchid has a distinctive flower designed to attract a different type of insect; the white flowers of the greater butterfly orchid are pollinated by moths with long tongues, while the pink flower heads of the pyramidal orchid are visited by butterflies. Bees and wasps are attracted to the flowers of early purple orchids, and the curiously-shaped bee orchid is visited by only one species of bumble bee which thinks that the flower is really another bee like itself!

Buttercups were once found in nearly every meadow, but they have suffered from the use of pesticide sprays and are no longer so common. Their leaves are poisonous, so grazing cattle and sheep leave them alone, but their shiny yellow flowers attract a variety of insects.

MEADOW BUTTERCUP

MEADOW PIPIT

YELLOWHAMMER

CORN BUNTING

LAPWING

SKYLARK

Swallows swoop low over meadows to catch the abundant insects which live there. When the swallows fly low, it is thought that rain is likely to fall before long; when the swallows fly high, the weather should remain fine for a while.

SWALLOW

A HOME FOR BIRDS

Many birds can find food and safe nesting sites in meadows. Seed-eaters like the corn bunting and yellowhammer feed on grass seeds, and sometimes search for other tasty items like insects, while skylarks and meadow pipits eat mostly insects but will also eat tiny worms, spiders and other small creatures. The lapwing uses its bill to probe into the surface of the soil and pull out tiny earthworms and slugs. Corn buntings and yellowhammers perch on bushes and posts to sing and attract mates, but the skylark soars high up over the meadow to sing its melodious song. The lapwing's squealing call is heard while it makes a swooping flight over its territory, its black and white wings making a striking pattern as it flies.

The skylark is a rather drab bird when seen close up; its streaked markings help it to blend in with dried grasses and bare earth, and are very helpful when it is resting on the ground, or being viewed from above by a predator. When it flies high up in the sky to sing, it is also very hard to see, but its song can be heard for a great distance.

COMMON BROOMRAPE

MEADOW CRANESBILL

41

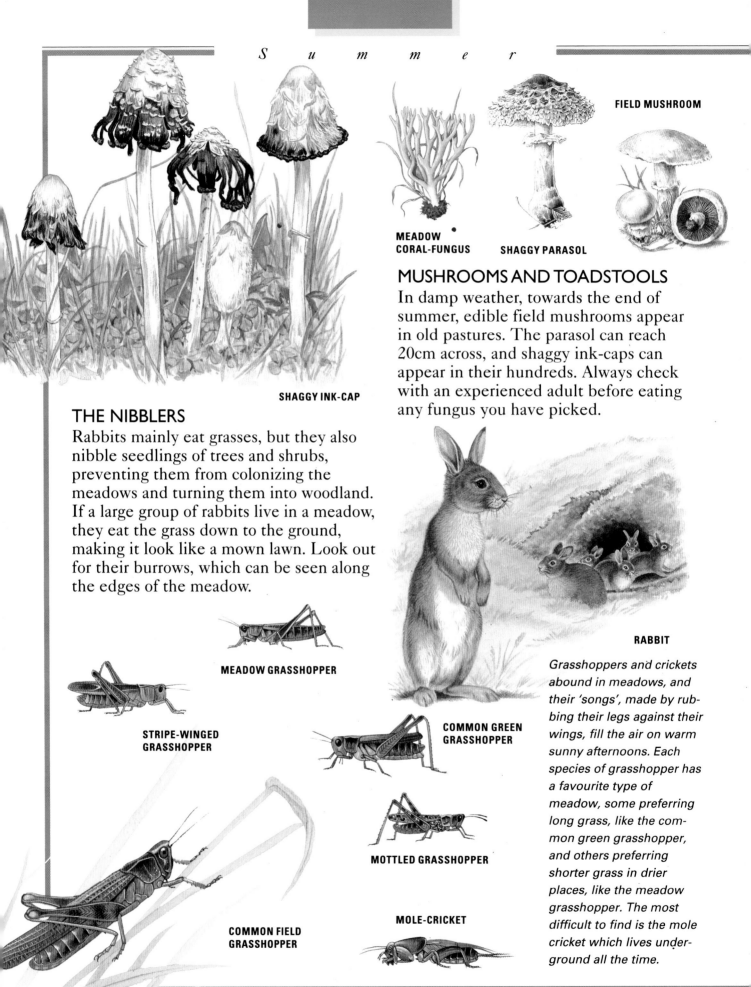

FIELD MUSHROOM

MEADOW CORAL-FUNGUS

SHAGGY PARASOL

SHAGGY INK-CAP

MUSHROOMS AND TOADSTOOLS

In damp weather, towards the end of summer, edible field mushrooms appear in old pastures. The parasol can reach 20cm across, and shaggy ink-caps can appear in their hundreds. Always check with an experienced adult before eating any fungus you have picked.

THE NIBBLERS

Rabbits mainly eat grasses, but they also nibble seedlings of trees and shrubs, preventing them from colonizing the meadows and turning them into woodland. If a large group of rabbits live in a meadow, they eat the grass down to the ground, making it look like a mown lawn. Look out for their burrows, which can be seen along the edges of the meadow.

RABBIT

MEADOW GRASSHOPPER

STRIPE-WINGED GRASSHOPPER

COMMON GREEN GRASSHOPPER

MOTTLED GRASSHOPPER

MOLE-CRICKET

COMMON FIELD GRASSHOPPER

Grasshoppers and crickets abound in meadows, and their 'songs', made by rubbing their legs against their wings, fill the air on warm sunny afternoons. Each species of grasshopper has a favourite type of meadow, some preferring long grass, like the common green grasshopper, and others preferring shorter grass in drier places, like the meadow grasshopper. The most difficult to find is the mole cricket which lives underground all the time.

THE LIFE OF A COPPER

Small copper butterflies are lively and flit from flower to flower, seldom stopping for long in one place. Their eggs and caterpillars are much more difficult to see, however, as they exactly match the colours of their food plants. The grub-like caterpillars of the small copper feed on docks and sorrel, and when fully grown they pupate, attaching the chrysalis to the plant by silk threads at the tail end. In a good year there may be three broods of small coppers.

SMALL COPPER

On sunny days, butterflies can be seen flying over the meadow visiting flowers for nectar, and looking for a mate

GRIZZLED SKIPPER

DINGY SKIPPER

LARGE SKIPPER

SMALL SKIPPER

SKIPPERS AND BLUES

The larvae of the skippers are very hard to see as they feed near the base of clumps of grass, dropping off on to the ground if disturbed. The adult butterflies have a lively darting flight and keep low amongst the grasses or short vegetation. The 'blues' are very attractive butterflies. Males usually have blue on their upper wings, and females are normally brown. Both sexes have spotted underwings, although the markings vary between species. Blues enjoy basking in the sun and may sometimes visit puddles for a drink.

GETTING CLOSER

Small skippers are found in grassy meadows, flying during July and August. They have an active, 'buzzing' flight, a lovely brown colour, and orangey brown tips to the antennae. You will need to get very close and not disturb the butterfly in order to tell which species you are looking at.

COMMON BLUE

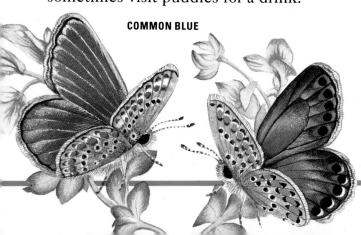

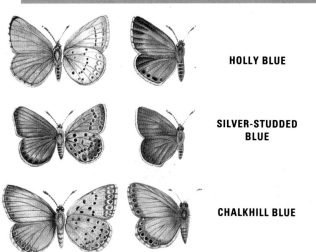

HOLLY BLUE

SILVER-STUDDED BLUE

CHALKHILL BLUE

SMALL BLUE

43

Heath & Moor

Heaths and moors are lonely, open places, where trees are scarce. Luckily, low bushes like gorse do grow here, and these provide a little shelter for birds and insects. Open, sandy patches make warm basking sites for reptiles, and the low vegetation makes it easy for them to find food.

NATTERJACK TOAD

The natterjack toad is easily recognized by the yellow stripe which runs down its back, and by its tendency to walk and climb rather than hop.

COMMON LIZARD

SAND LIZARD

SPAWNING, SUNNING AND EATING

Reptiles abound on heaths and moors, but amphibians are less common unless there are some pools for them to spawn in. Natterjack toads are rarely found away from sandy heaths, preferring to spawn in shallow pools which become warm in summer. The handsome sand lizard, with its green neck, hides under vegetation for much of the time, but enjoys sunning itself on sheltered banks. The common lizard is less colourful, but also enjoys sunbathing, sometimes being seen on top of a fallen log or a stone. Lizards are sometimes eaten by snakes; both the smooth snake and the adder will eat them, although adders will take small mammals as well.

Adders are identified by zig-zag markings down the back, and a V-shaped mark on the head. They also look quite fat, with a short pointed tail. The eye has a vertical pupil, but most people avoid getting that near to a venomous snake! Smooth snakes lack the V mark, and also have a longer, pointed tail.

ADDER

SMOOTH SNAKE

HEN HARRIER

STONECHAT

THE FAMOUS ACTOR

Golden plovers nest on remote, boggy moorlands. When sitting on the nest they are extremely difficult to spot, but if they leave the nest they will move off looking as if they are injured, dragging one wing and making a plaintive cry. This is intended to lead a predator such as a fox away from the nest. If you see a bird doing this, it should be left alone as a real predator may find the unattended nest and steal the eggs or chicks.

S   W

GOLDEN PLOVER

PEACE AND QUIET

High moorlands provide safe nesting conditions for birds which nest on the ground, such as golden plover and curlew. There are so few people and predators there that they can usually raise their young in safety. Red grouse are found nowhere else, feeding exclusively on heather shoots. Smaller birds, like the stonechat, linnet and Dartford warbler, use the cover of gorse bushes for safety, but the predatory hen harrier nests on the ground. Great grey shrikes perch on the top of bushes or posts looking for small mammals and birds to feed on. They are only winter visitors to heathlands in Britain.

DARTFORD WARBLER

GREAT GREY SHRIKE

LINNET

The nightjar is the most difficult heathland bird to see because of its superb camouflage and habit of sitting perfectly still on the ground, even when approached.

NIGHTJAR

CURLEW

RED GROUSE

45

ORB-WEB SPIDER

BOG BUSH CRICKET

Bog bush crickets live amongst cross-leaved heath in the damper parts of heaths. These very lively insects feed on plants and other small insects. Females have a long curved ovipostor for laying eggs.

EMPEROR MOTH

The male emperor moth is a very colourful insect, with bold markings on its wings and large, branched antennae. If disturbed from vegetation during the day, it flies rapidly away to a safe place.

TRAPS FOR INSECTS

Heaths and moors are excellent places for finding insects, but there are many hidden dangers for them. The beautiful webs of orb web spiders, strung between gorse bushes or heather clumps, show up well on dewy mornings in late summer, and they may reveal the insects the spider has caught. Insects which escape the spider's web may be caught by an insect-eating plant, the sundew, which grows in boggy places and traps small insects on its glistening sticky leaves.

COMMON SUNDEW

YORKSHIRE FOG

COMMON GORSE

THE POD THAT GOES 'POP'

On hot, sunny afternoons the ripe seed pods of gorse shrivel up and then burst open with a 'pop', scattering seeds around the bush. Spread newspaper, or a white sheet, around a gorse bush, leave it for a few hours and then look for the seeds which have been spread by the bursting pods.

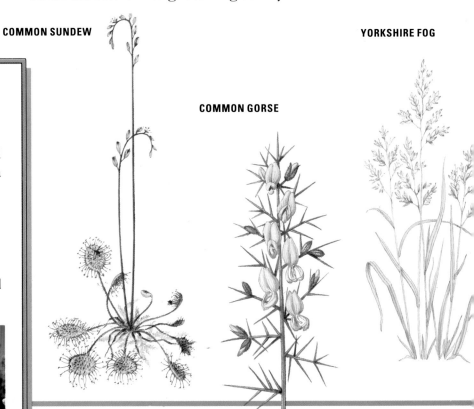

THE TOUGH SURVIVORS

Heaths and moors usually have poorly drained soils lacking in the nutrients most plants need for healthy growth, so only a few species are able to flourish there. Tough grasses like the purple moor grass, Yorkshire fog and sheep's fescue can cope with acid soils, and grow well when other plants would just wither away. Bracken is a tough fern which quickly colonizes heaths and moors, especially in the drier places, and where there is heavy grazing by sheep.

WARNING!

Sundew is common in the wetter parts of moors and heaths, and is often found growing at the edge of peaty pools. Look for it in damp hollows and near the edges of streams. Take care wherever you see sundew - the ground is probably very boggy indeed.

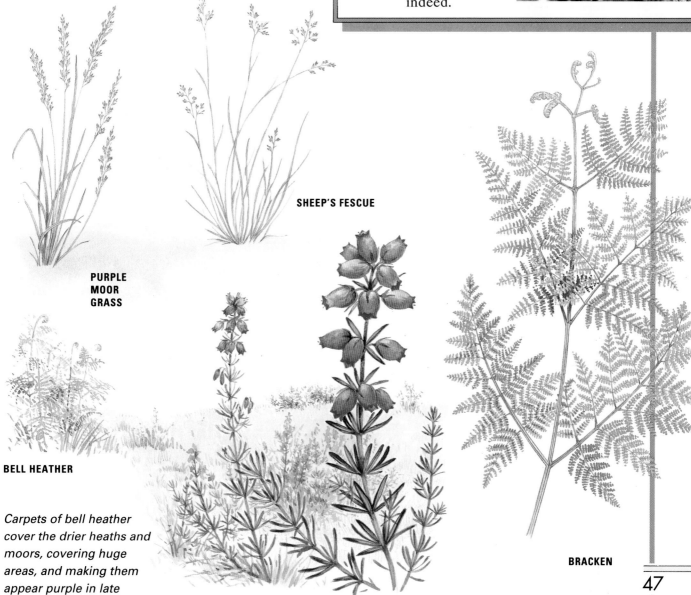

SHEEP'S FESCUE

PURPLE MOOR GRASS

BELL HEATHER

BRACKEN

Carpets of bell heather cover the drier heaths and moors, covering huge areas, and making them appear purple in late summer.

Seashore

Mid-summer is the height of the breeding season for seabirds. A visit to the coast is very exciting, as so many birds which normally live far out to sea will be seen nesting, fishing, flying to and fro or just resting near the shore. This is the best time to see coastal flowers, too, as many of the most colourful species bloom in summer.

CODE OF CONDUCT

Ground-nesting seabirds like terns should never be approached closely as there is a risk that they will leave their nests; eggs or chicks will then be exposed to predators or bad weather. Keep a safe distance away from the nest, move slowly and be as quiet as possible when close to nesting seabirds, and take great care on steep cliffs.

EIDER ♀ ♂

SHAG W S juv

The large, colourful beak of the puffin is only present in the summer; in winter most of it falls off, leaving a smaller, less colourful bill like the juvenile's. Puffins use their strange bill for attracting a mate, fighting, excavating a nesting burrow and catching fish.

juv

CHANGING COLOURS

The male and female eider ducks have quite different plumage; females are a drab brown, making them very difficult to see when they are sitting tight on their nests, but males are boldly marked with black and white. Young eider ducks have the same colourings as their mothers when they are first taken to sea. The shag is normally a rather drab bird, but for a short time in summer its plumage has a beautiful green gloss, it has a crest on its head, and its eyes are an attractive shade of green.

FULMAR

GANNET

ARCTIC TERN

GUILLEMOT

W

S

Many birds find their food in the open sea. Both terns and gannets plunge-dive for fish, while guillemots swim after fish underwater, using their wings like flippers, and fulmars pick food from the surface.

FLOWERS OF THE COAST

In summer, cliff-tops are carpeted with many shades of pink thrift, growing well in the most exposed conditions. Wild pansies are more delicate, and they prefer the shelter of other plants amongst the sand dunes. The tough, prickly leaves of sea holly protect it from damage and the drying effects of the wind on the sandy shores it grows on. Sea lavender is most common on salt marshes, but some species also grow on rocky cliffs, proving a great attraction to migrant butterflies.

SEA LAVENDER

SEA HOLLY

WILD PANSY

The long roots of thrift mean that it can reach water far below the surface. This helps it survive in dry places, such as on cliffs.

THRIFT

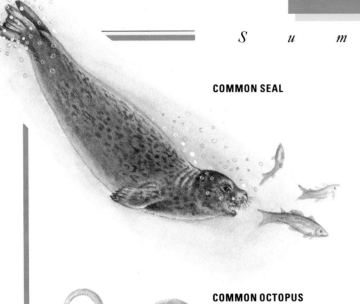

COMMON SEAL

SAND CREATURES

A sandy shore hides many worms, shellfish and shrimps. Many creatures have breathing holes on the surface and some leave casts of sand as well.

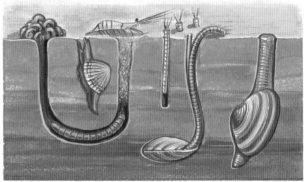

COMMON OCTOPUS

PROTECTION AND FEEDING

Common seals rest on sandy beaches at low tide, but when the tide is in, they chase fish for food. Both the squid and the octopus feed on crabs and shrimps which emerge from their sandy hiding places when covered by the tide. Shore crabs often bury themselves, leaving their hiding places to feed when they feel safe. The octopus and squid can both change their colours to match their surroundings, making them very hard to see. The spiny spider crab is protected by its thick spiny shell; it may disguise itself by sticking tiny pieces of seaweed to its shell. With its sharp-pointed pincers it is able to pick tiny pieces of food out of the sand.

COMMON SQUID

SPINY SPIDER CRAB

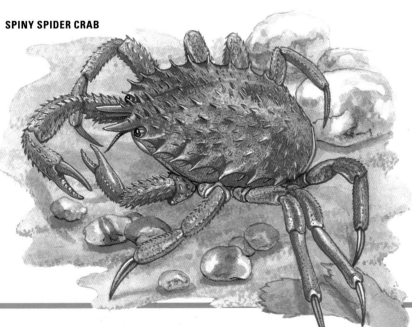

SHORE CRAB

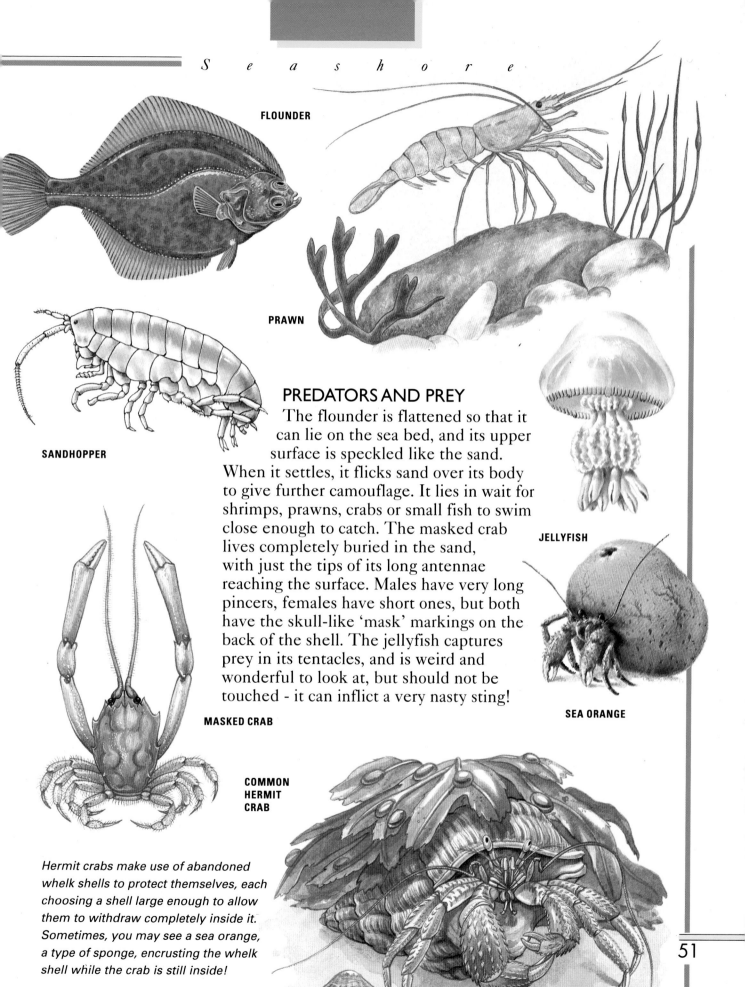

FLOUNDER

PRAWN

SANDHOPPER

JELLYFISH

SEA ORANGE

MASKED CRAB

COMMON
HERMIT
CRAB

PREDATORS AND PREY

The flounder is flattened so that it can lie on the sea bed, and its upper surface is speckled like the sand. When it settles, it flicks sand over its body to give further camouflage. It lies in wait for shrimps, prawns, crabs or small fish to swim close enough to catch. The masked crab lives completely buried in the sand, with just the tips of its long antennae reaching the surface. Males have very long pincers, females have short ones, but both have the skull-like 'mask' markings on the back of the shell. The jellyfish captures prey in its tentacles, and is weird and wonderful to look at, but should not be touched - it can inflict a very nasty sting!

Hermit crabs make use of abandoned whelk shells to protect themselves, each choosing a shell large enough to allow them to withdraw completely inside it. Sometimes, you may see a sea orange, a type of sponge, encrusting the whelk shell while the crab is still inside!

51

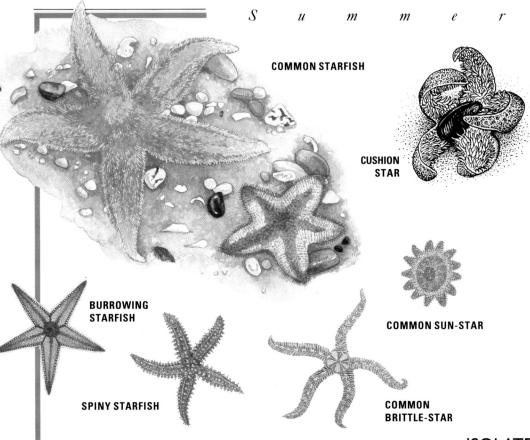

COMMON STARFISH

CUSHION STAR

Starfish open their prey by pulling on the two halves of the shell. They can keep up pressure for several hours, and eventually the mollusc can resist no longer, and the shell opens.

BEADLET ANEMONE

BURROWING STARFISH

SPINY STARFISH

COMMON SUN-STAR

COMMON BRITTLE-STAR

Starfish all have five arms and a spiny body, but they vary greatly in size, colour, length of spines and habits. Burrowing starfish are hard to find as they live buried in sand, but spiny starfish, cushion stars and small brittle-stars can be found in rock pools.

ISOLATED ROCK POOLS

A rock pool is a tiny world of its own, cut off from the sea by the falling tide. For a few hours, until the tide returns, no creatures can leave, and none will enter, except perhaps hungry birds or inquisitive people. Grazing molluscs like periwinkles and limpets move around in the pool scraping algae off the rocks with their rough tongues, but the filter-feeding mussels remain in one place, fixed by tough threads.

They may be attacked by dog whelks which burrow through their shells and suck out the contents.

COMMON LIMPET

FLAT PERIWINKLE

EDIBLE PERIWINKLE

COMMON WHELK

Beautiful, but deadly, sea anemones feed by trapping fish and shrimps in their stinging tentacles. Beadlet anemones are colourful with blue beadlets in a ring around the tentacles. The parasitic anemone is always found with shells occupied by hermit crabs, and helps protect them.

SEA LETTUCE

SPIRAL OR FLAT WRACK

PARASITIC ANEMONE

SERRATED WRACK

KNOTTED OR EGG WRACK

SEAWEEDS

On the rocks surrounding the rock pool, a curtain of seaweeds can be found. When exposed to the air, the seaweeds hang limply over the rocks, but when underwater they float upwards showing their attractive shapes and colours.

LICHENS

Rocks near the high-tide line sometimes look as if they have been painted orange or black; these colours are really patches of lichens, slow-growing plants which grow on bare rocks where no other plants could survive.

LICHEN

Caloplaca marina

Verrucaria maura

Anaptychia fusca

INVESTIGATING ROCK POOLS

The best rock pools to study are large deep ones, but take care near them. Shallow pools, high up on the shore, become too hot for many creatures to survive in, but deep pools, lower down the shore, will remain cool and allow far more creatures to survive while the tide is out. Use a long-handled net to search for creatures in the deep pools, but remember to return them to the pool.

Lecanora atra

Xanthoria parietina

River

Water levels may be low in a river in mid-summer, as hot sunny weather and lack of rain dry up the land. Many fish breed in the summer, and most are able to find plenty of food since insects, molluscs and crustaceans are abundant in fine weather.

BULLHEAD

THREE-SPINED STICKLEBACK

FIERCE FISH

The bullhead and stickleback are both small fish, but they are very well equipped to find food and look after themselves. Bullheads have spines on their gill covers, and sticklebacks have spines on their backs. These are a deterrent to other fish which may try to eat them. Bullheads usually hide under stones, darting out to catch prey when it is swept past by the current. Sticklebacks prefer to hide in weed and chase their prey through the open water. The crayfish is a lobster-like crustacean which hides under stones in clean rivers, emerging at night to feed on worms, snails and fish eggs.

River limpets attach themselves to stones in fast water, using their powerful 'foot' and pointing their shells into the current to reduce drag. They graze on algae coating the stones, and clamp down firmly at the first sign of danger.

A CLOSER LOOK

To get a closer look at small fish and animals, use a long-handled net. Searching among weeds near to the river bank will yield the best results, but always make sure you don't go to rivers alone. Never paddle in the water unless you can see the bottom, and are sure the water is free from pollution. Once you have looked at your 'catch', return everything to the river.

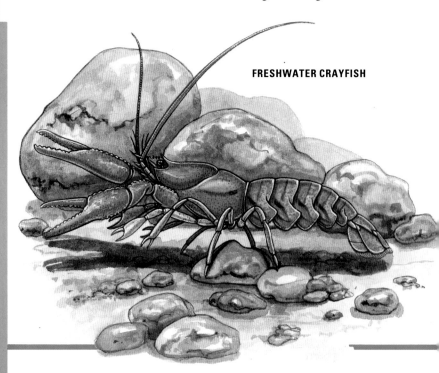

FRESHWATER CRAYFISH

WATER LOUSE

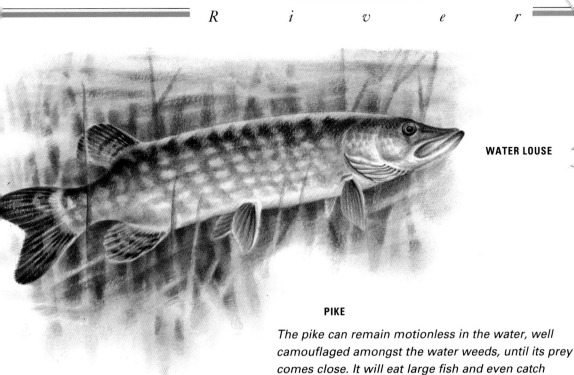

PIKE

The pike can remain motionless in the water, well camouflaged amongst the water weeds, until its prey comes close. It will eat large fish and even catch ducklings and water voles for food.

FISH OF CLEAN WATER

Both the brown trout and the minnow like clean water, so they are usually found in fast-flowing rivers which are free from pollution. Trout are streamlined, fast-swimming fish which eat other smaller fish and are especially fond of aquatic insects like mayflies and caddis flies, which they catch at the surface. Minnows live in large shoals, feeding on tiny water creatures like the water louse, and sometimes being caught themselves by trout.

BROWN TROUT

MINNOW

The fish leech attaches itself to the bodies of fish, sucks their blood until it is full, then drops off. When it needs another meal, it reaches out and sticks to a passing fish.

The cyclops is a common, one-eyed water flea which carries its eggs around in two sacs beside its tail. It is a favourite food of many small fish.

FISH LEECH

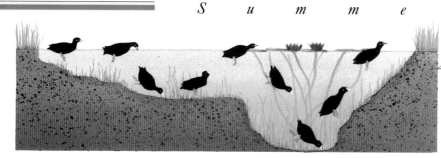

COOT

GREY WAGTAIL

YELLOW WAGTAIL

♂

♀

WATERSIDE BIRDS

Rivers attract birds because there is so much food available to them. Some, like the coot, can feed at the water's edge and make shallow dives to reach food which other birds could not find. The attractive wagtails feed at the edge of the river on insects which they pick from stones and plants. Grey wagtails perch on stones in the water and nest under old bridges. Yellow wagtails nest in grassy meadows near rivers and feed on insects on the river banks.

THE SECRETIVE BITTERN

Rivers with reed beds along their banks attract the bittern, a large heron-like bird which is very difficult to see. It gives itself away when it makes its deep booming call in the breeding season, and occasionally it flies low over the reeds to a new feeding spot. However, for most of the time it stands patiently in the reeds waiting for its prey, which may be anything from fish to frogs to baby birds which come close enough to catch.

KINGFISHER

BITTERN

BLUE-AND-ORANGE FLASH

One of the most beautiful and colourful birds is the kingfisher, but it can be very difficult to see until it flies. It makes a shrill whistle as it flies over the river and a gentle splash as it dives in for a fish.

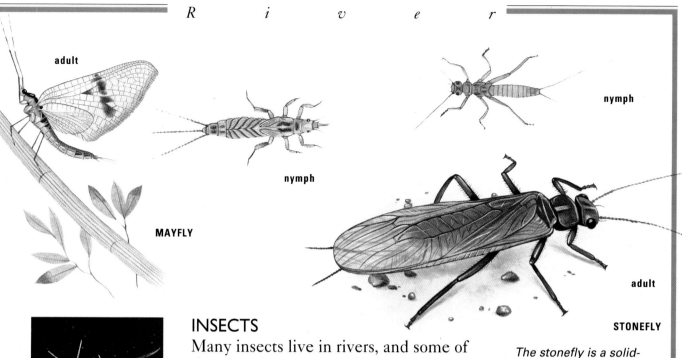

adult

nymph

MAYFLY

nymph

adult

STONEFLY

INSECTS

Many insects live in rivers, and some of them can be very troublesome to humans. Mosquitoes pester people and animals on summer evenings, hoping to extract a meal of blood! Stoneflies and mayflies are only found in the cleanest of water; their nymphs live underwater, feeding on algae, and the adults emerge to live for a short time in the air before laying their eggs and then dying. Banded demoiselles are also found only in clean water. On sunny afternoons they flit over the riverside vegetation like shiny metallic butterflies, the females dipping into the water to lay their eggs.

Mayfly nymphs will spend about one year developing underwater, feeding on microscopic plants. They have leaf-like gills along the sides of their bodies to help them take in oxygen.

The stonefly is a solid-looking insect with bold veins marking its wings. Its nymph has two tails, whereas the mayfly nymph has three.

MOSQUITO

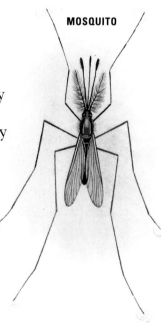

♂

♀

nymph

BANDED DEMOISELLE DAMSELFLY

Mosquitoes feed on blood, and find this by piercing the skin of mammals, especially humans. In some countries they carry malaria, but in Europe they are free from this disease.

57

Crack willow grows on river banks, and its bright red roots stick out into the water.

CRACK WILLOW

GROWING WILLOWS

Willows grow easily from cuttings. Snap off some twigs and put them in damp soil in a flower pot. They will soon produce roots and shoots if they are kept watered.

WATER CROWFOOT

Osiers are willows which can be 'pollarded', or cut back to stumps every year. They produce long stems called 'willow wands', useful for weaving and making baskets.

RIVERSIDE PLANTS

Willow trees grow well on river banks in places where other trees would find conditions too wet. Some will have been planted there to provide useful timber, but others will have been spread by small twigs taking root in the bank. Yellow flag irises grow on the river-bank, making a spectacular display in summer; their large yellow flowers stand out above the tops of the other vegetation. Yellow loosestrife has branched clusters of smaller yellow flowers and black dots on its leaves, and is harder to find. Reedmace produces strange brown flowers on the end of tall waving stems which may be used as perches for dragonflies or even kingfishers.

Water crowfoot is a type of buttercup with white flowers and rounded, floating leaves. It also has submerged leaves which look like fine branches.

YELLOW LOOSESTRIFE

REEDMACE

YELLOW FLAG IRIS

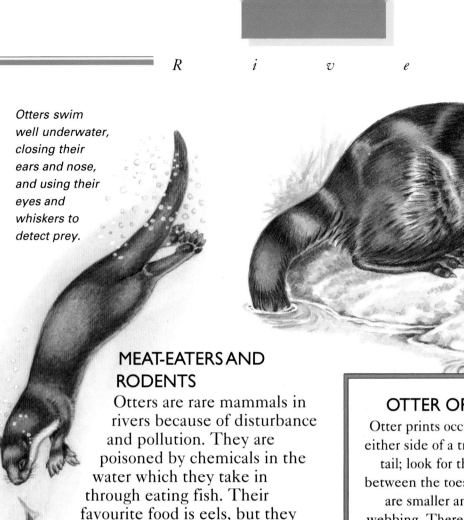

OTTER

Otters swim well underwater, closing their ears and nose, and using their eyes and whiskers to detect prey.

MEAT-EATERS AND RODENTS

Otters are rare mammals in rivers because of disturbance and pollution. They are poisoned by chemicals in the water which they take in through eating fish. Their favourite food is eels, but they will also eat other fish, crayfish, small birds and mammals, and even water insects. Otters are very shy of humans and have nocturnal habits, so they are difficult to see. They live in a 'holt', a hole in a very well-concealed place on the river-bank. They may be confused with mink, especially when they are swimming, but mink are only half the size and have more pointed heads. The much smaller water vole is a rodent. It lives in holes in the river-bank, emerging every hour or so to feed on water plants. The mink is one of its greatest enemies.

OTTER OR MINK?

Otter prints occur in pairs on either side of a trail left by the tail; look for the webbing between the toes. Mink prints are smaller and lack the webbing. There is also no tail mark. A good place to look for these tracks is in the mud of an estuary.

Otter prints

Mink prints

Wild mink are usually dark brown, but those in fur farms have the more attractive pastel colours of grey or light brown.

EUROPEAN MINK

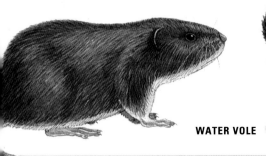

WATER VOLE

59

Pond

Ponds are excellent places for wildlife, and in mid-summer they are teeming with life. Insects abound, both in the water and above it, and snails are to be seen slowly feeding on the pond weeds.

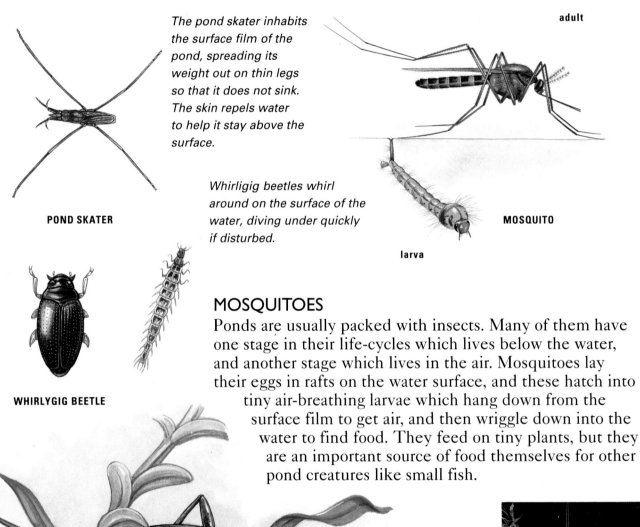

The pond skater inhabits the surface film of the pond, spreading its weight out on thin legs so that it does not sink. The skin repels water to help it stay above the surface.

POND SKATER

adult

Whirligig beetles whirl around on the surface of the water, diving under quickly if disturbed.

MOSQUITO

larva

WHIRLYGIG BEETLE

MOSQUITOES

Ponds are usually packed with insects. Many of them have one stage in their life-cycles which lives below the water, and another stage which lives in the air. Mosquitoes lay their eggs in rafts on the water surface, and these hatch into tiny air-breathing larvae which hang down from the surface film to get air, and then wriggle down into the water to find food. They feed on tiny plants, but they are an important source of food themselves for other pond creatures like small fish.

WATER SCORPION

Water scorpions are fierce pond insects which catch other pond creatures with their pincer-like front legs. They breathe through a long tube at the tail end.

GREAT DIVING BEETLE

Great diving beetle larvae breathe air, so must make regular trips to the surface, drawing in air through the tail end. They feed on other larvae and small fish.

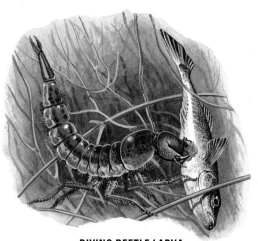

DIVING BEETLE LARVA

GREAT SILVER BEETLE

DIVING BEETLES AND WATER BOATMEN

Diving beetles are common in ponds. Some are fierce predators like the handsome great diving beetle which catches fish, tadpoles and other larvae. Both the adult beetle and the larva are predators. The great silver beetle is our largest water beetle and is a plant eater, preferring weedy ponds with lots of ivy-leaved duckweed in them. Its larva is another fierce carnivore, feeding on fish, tadpoles and snails.

Water boatmen are bugs which mostly feed on other pond creatures; they have piercing mouth parts strong enough to penetrate human skin. Some swim upside down, and feed on insects trapped in the surface film.

WATER BOATMAN

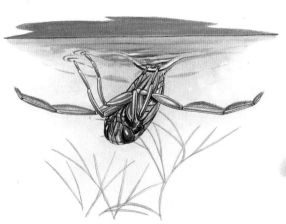

GREAT POND SNAIL

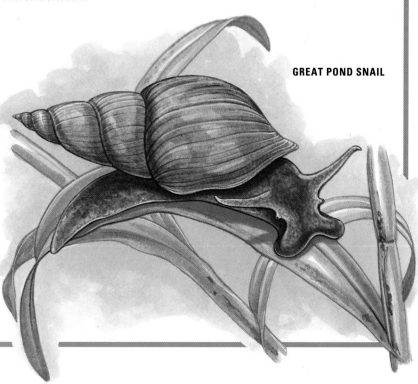

The great pond snail is our largest pond snail, up to 5cm long. Its shell is sharply pointed and the shell has a large mouth. The snail moves slowly around the pond feeding on plants, but will also scavenge on dead fish. It is most common in ponds where there is plenty of calcium to help form its shell in the water.

COMMON FROG

BREEDING IN PONDS

Frogs and toads can live on land but they must both return to water to breed. In spring, frogs return to their breeding ponds to spawn where they may gather in hundreds. They will stay near the pond in summer, especially in very hot weather. The eggs hatch into tadpoles which feed on pond weeds at first, and then move on to animal matter as they get larger.

COMMON TOAD

GOLDFISH

THE LEATHERY TOAD

Toads spend less time in water than frogs. Their leathery skin helps them retain water in their bodies so they can stay on land for longer periods. The warts on their skin give off a poison which discourages predators from eating them. Garden ponds are excellent habitats for frogs and toads, as long as they don't have goldfish in them. Goldfish eat large numbers of tadpoles, and in a small pond there will be nowhere for them to hide.

CANADIAN PONDWEED

DUCKWEED

Canadian pondweed is a useful plant in a pond as it releases oxygen into the water on sunny days, and provides food for fish and pond snails.

The rich flowers of purple loosestrife are a great attraction for butterflies.

PURPLE LOOSESTRIFE

Duckweed forms a floating green carpet on the surface of a pond, providing shelter for small creatures beneath it.

PALMATE NEWT

LAYING EGGS

Newts lay their eggs singly, protecting each one in a leaf. Toads produce a long string of spawn, twining it around plant stems to keep it in place, but frogs produce a large mass of jelly, with each round egg in a separate layer of jelly. Study the spawn in a clear container, but always put it back in the pond.

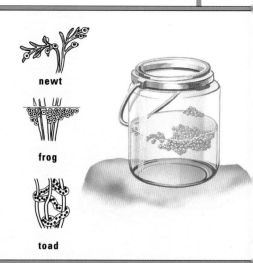

newt

frog

toad

The male palmate newt is easily recognized as it has webbed hind feet and a tiny bristle on the end of its tail.

Dragonfly nymphs are active predators, feeding on other underwater insects, but they also eat many tadpoles and small fish.

COMMON HAWKER

nymph

adult

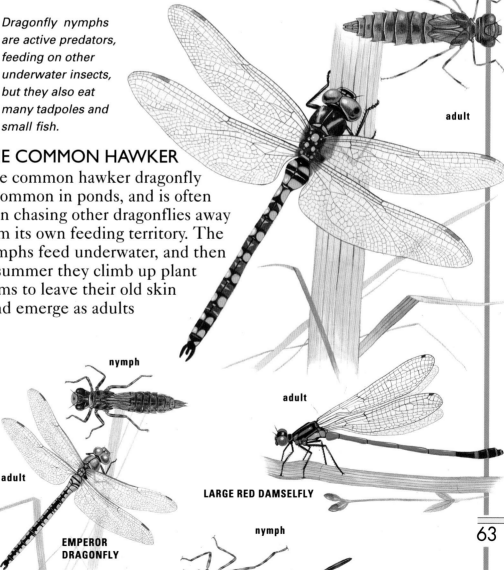

THE COMMON HAWKER

The common hawker dragonfly is common in ponds, and is often seen chasing other dragonflies away from its own feeding territory. The nymphs feed underwater, and then in summer they climb up plant stems to leave their old skin and emerge as adults

nymph

adult

BLUE-TAILED DAMSELFLY

LARGE RED DAMSELFLY

adult

The emperor dragonfly is easily recognized by its deep blue colour and powerful flight.

EMPEROR DRAGONFLY

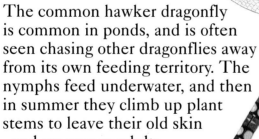

nymph

Farmland

Farmland is used to produce food for humans, but it also provides food and homes for many birds and mammals. Some of these are the farmer's friends because they help control pests, but others are a nuisance because they eat his crops. There is always plenty of wildlife to be seen on a farm in summer.

BLACK KITE

BARN OWL

LITTLE OWL

BIRDS OF FARMLAND

Rooks and crows are both large black birds, but are easy to tell apart. Rooks have a white face and pointed bill, and look as if they are wearing baggy trousers, while crows are all black with a larger bill. Rooks usually live in large noisy groups, but crows are only seen in ones and twos. Black kites are large birds of prey, rare in Britain, which are seen circling over farmland and towns looking for carrion to scavenge. The ghostly white barn owl is a rare sight, found only on farms where there are quiet barns to nest in and rough fields to hunt for voles and mice. Little owls are much smaller and sit out on fence posts in the day showing their scowling faces and large yellow eyes.

Pheasants like to live on the ground in very open places. They especially like farmlands, open woodlands and heaths.

ROOK

CARRION CROW

PHEASANT

♀

♂

MALE AND FEMALE

Pheasant males and females have different markings, so it should be easy to tell them apart. The female is a dull, brown colour with darker brown speckles, whereas the male is a much more colourful bird, with a dark green and red head, and a beautiful bronze body.

BANK VOLE

FIELD VOLE

COMMON SHREW

SMALL MAMMALS OF FARMLAND

Voles are very common on farmland. Field voles have short tails and live in grassy meadows where they nibble roots and shoots. Their nests are made of shredded grass and may be found in long grass (see above) or under sheets of corrugated iron. Bank voles have longer tails and are a richer brown colour; they prefer to live in hedgerows and copses where they feed on fruits and seeds. Shrews are insect feeders, and have longer tails, pointed noses and smaller eyes. Harvest mice are very small and make their tiny nests in corn stems. Their long tails help them clamber through the corn.

Look out! The largest mammal of farmland is the bull, which may be wandering freely in a field. If it is in a field with a footpath, it should be safe to cross, but don't take any risks or do anything which will startle it.

HARE

HARVEST MICE

The long hind legs of the hare help it run to safety at high speed if disturbed. The black-tipped ears and large eyes are distinctive.

POPPIES

Poppies are very distinctive, bright red flowers. Their capsules are like pepper pots, designed to scatter the seeds living inside them as they are shaken by the wind. They grow on the end of long stalks which wave about as the wind blows, and the seeds are very easily spread around.

COMMON POPPY

Common poppy

Long-headed poppy

Bristly poppy

Pale poppy

THE TREE BARRIER

Trees were planted in hedge-rows to keep animals from straying, to provide shelter, and as a useful source of timber. Wych elms produce large bunches of winged seeds, whereas the winged seeds of the field maple are produced in pairs. Weeping willows grow easily if planted, so often end up in hedges and boundaries. Blackthorn is a very useful hedgerow tree as it is very prickly, soon making a barrier which humans and animals cannot get through.

Sloes are very sour to taste, but are eaten by birds and small mammals. They are usually covered with a pale blue dust of yeast cells.

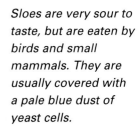

WYCH ELM

FIELD MAPLE

WEEPING WILLOW

BLACKTHORN

COMMON SPOTTED ORCHID

WHITE CLOVER

SCARLET PIMPERNEL

COMMON TOADFLAX

The common toadflax has yellow flowers with an orange centre, and flowers between June and October each year.

FARMLAND FLOWERS

Although much of the countryside is intensively farmed, there are still plenty of places where wild flowers can be found. Old pastures, field edges, hedgerows, lanes and old tracks are all worth exploring. The 'poor man's weather glass', or scarlet pimpernel, is common along tracks where its flowers close to warn of approaching rain. White clover can be abundant in meadows, and is a good source of nectar to bees. The yellow spikes of toadflax are easily spotted in hedgerows, but the pink spikes of the common spotted orchid are harder to find as this plant is becoming more scarce.

The beautiful blue cornflower was once abundant in cornfields, but has now almost vanished because of weed-killers.

CORNFLOWER

OX-EYE DAISY

Ox-eye daisies have large daisy-like flowers with a yellow centre borne on long stalks. They are very common in some old pastures and along roadsides.

CORN MARIGOLD

This was once a very common flower, but, like the blue cornflower, has almost vanished. It still grows in a few places where the farming is more traditional and where the soils are sandy and slightly acid. It can completely fill some fields with golden-orange patches of colour. Look for it around the edges of fields in late summer.

Park & Garden

A flower-filled garden is a pleasant place to sit in mid-summer. The flowers attract many insects, especially butterflies and hoverflies, and if the gardener does not use too many pesticides there will be plenty of other insects as well, many of them the gardener's friends.

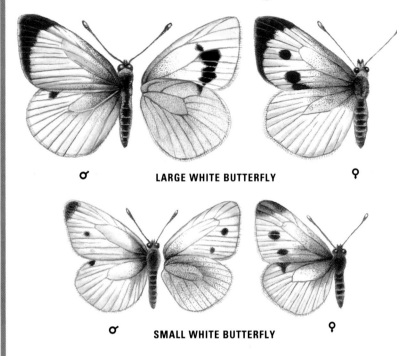

♂ **LARGE WHITE BUTTERFLY** ♀

♂ **SMALL WHITE BUTTERFLY** ♀

GARDEN BUTTERFLIES

A park or garden with plenty of flowers in it is an attraction to butterflies; they visit flowers for nectar and help to pollinate them. The butterflies will also look for suitable plants on which to lay their eggs, so when the caterpillars emerge they will have something to feed on. Some of the butterflies, like the large white, are not very welcome, as their caterpillars feed on garden crops like cabbage, but others, like the small tortoiseshell, lay their eggs on stinging nettles.

♂ **SMALL TORTOISESHELL BUTTERFLY** ♀

The larva of the ladybird is a fierce creature with powerful jaws which it uses to catch aphids. It moves slowly along plant stems eating several aphids in a day, so it is one of the gardener's friends as aphids are pests which destroy some plants.

SEVEN-SPOT LADYBIRD

♂ **COMMA BUTTERFLY** ♀

Adult 7-spot ladybirds are common in gardens, and are easily recognizable because of their distinctive red and black markings.

LADYBIRD LARVA

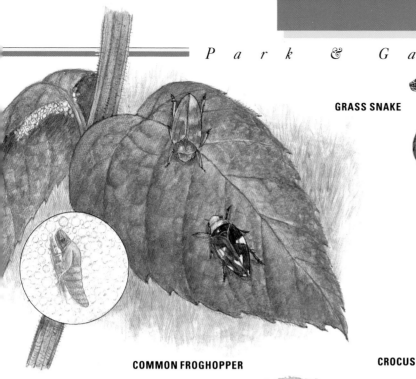

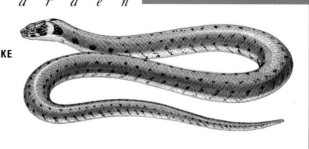

GRASS SNAKE

WILD DAFFODIL

CROCUS

COMMON FROGHOPPER

COCKCHAFER BEETLE

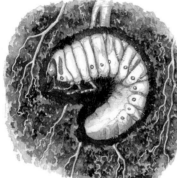

COCKCHAFER LARVA

The large white grub of the cockchafer larva lives underground and feeds on tree roots.

COMMON WASP

GARDEN VISITORS

The harmless grass snake is an unusual visitor to the garden, but is fond of ponds where it can find fish and frogs to eat, and compost heaps where it may lay its eggs. Wasps are unwelcome, but they are really good for the garden because in early summer they eat the grubs of garden pests, and later in the year they eat rotten fruit which no-one really wants. Froghoppers are small insects which suck the sap from plants and hide themselves in a patch of foam.

THE LURE OF ROTTING FRUIT

In summer, wasps love to eat fruit which is rotting on the ground, and will compete with other insects such as flies to get it. Their powerful mouth parts are used to bite into the fruit, which is used as a substitute for nectar.

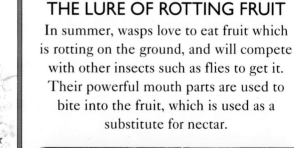

BUFF-TAILED BUMBLE BEE

69

JAY

ANTING

Jays have the curious habit of anting, or allowing ants to crawl all over them. A jay will stand on the ground on a large lawn where there are plenty of ants; it adopts a strange position with its wings half open and touching the ground, its neck stretched up and its head bent down. It will pick up some ants and place them on its feathers; others will crawl on it from the ground. This strange behaviour may help to keep the plumage in good order as the ants release formic acid, and may help kill ticks and fleas.

juv

SONG THRUSH

juv

SPOTTED FLYCATCHER

THE GREATEST VARIETY

Visiting a park will present you with a great number and variety of trees, most of which should be labelled for easy identification. Visit a local park and see how many you can recognize.

WEEPING JAPANESE CHERRY

SMOOTH JAPANESE MAPLE

INDIAN BEAN TREE

GINKGO

HORSE CHESTNUT

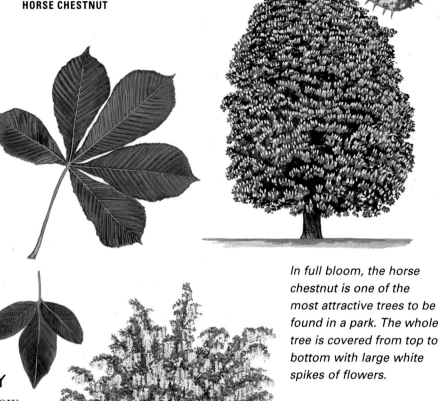

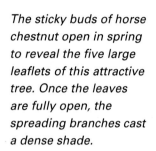

The sticky buds of horse chestnut open in spring to reveal the five large leaflets of this attractive tree. Once the leaves are fully open, the spreading branches cast a dense shade.

In full bloom, the horse chestnut is one of the most attractive trees to be found in a park. The whole tree is covered from top to bottom with large white spikes of flowers.

BEAUTIFUL BUT DEADLY

The beautiful hanging yellow flower spikes of laburnum form dry seed pods containing small black seeds. These are very poisonous, and have been known to kill fish by falling into a pond. The leaves of the laburnum look very much like clover leaves.

LABURNUM

SOUR CHERRY

SOUR CHERRY

The mass of white blossom of the sour cherry tree is followed by bunches of red cherries in late summer. These are the Morello cherries used in jam and fruit drinks. Some cherries have beautiful blossom but don't produce edible fruits.

71

Town

Towns provide homes for several plants and animals which have learnt to live alongside people. They may be quite harmless, like the tiger moths, helpful like the bats which eat troublesome insects, or a nuisance like the house mouse. People's pets, such as cats and dogs, also live in towns, and they may have an effect on what sorts of wildlife are found there.

TABBY CAT

PIPISTRELLE BAT

Tabby cats are common in towns. Some may be pets, but many will be strays, finding their own food and living in old buildings and garden sheds. The strays catch mice and small birds, and scavenge for scraps.

This colony of young long-eared bats are living in the loft of a house, and await the twilight with excitement, as they will soon be able to go out into the dark in search of food.

A COMMON BAT

The pipistrelle bat is one of the smallest bats, but also one of the most common. They like to roost in houses, hiding in lofts, in cavity walls and under roof tiles, and are often found in large groups. Houses have become more important to them as natural roosting sites in woodlands become scarce. Pipistrelles leave their roosts early in the evening, often flying before it gets really dark. They eat large numbers of insects, including troublesome pests like midges, and the young are born in mid-summer.

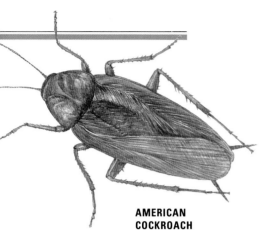

AMERICAN COCKROACH

COMMON EARWIG

Earwigs and cockroaches are commonly found in towns. The earwig feeds on plant matter and small insects, while the cockroach only feeds on dead plant matter. Both are considered pests.

HOUSE MICE

House mice will eat almost anything that humans eat, and can quickly gnaw their way through wood, thin metal and plastic, so very few food containers will keep them out. They are small enough to squeeze through gaps in brickwork or under doors, so they can easily get into larders. They are rather smelly and spoil more food than they eat, so people always try to get rid of them. Even with cats, traps and poison, mice are still widespread in towns.

House mice are very good climbers and can get around a house very easily by climbing up the inside of cavity walls, or by scrambling up curtains. They are most active in the dark and when they think no one is around. They make permanent runways and burrows, scented with urine.

BREEDING

House mice are able to breed all through the year. They make nests in quiet places away from their main runs. If they cannot find any natural bedding such as dried grass, they will chew up paper or rags to line their nests. Litters may be large, and a female mouse can produce several litters in one year. At first the young are blind and hairless, but they gradually develop the mousy brown colourings of the adult.

HOUSE MOUSE

GARDEN TIGER MOTH

THE HAIRY CATERPILLAR

Garden tiger moths are striking and colourful, warning predators to leave them alone by their bold markings. The caterpillars are very hairy, and when disturbed drop to the ground and roll into a ball so that the whole body surface looks hairy. The hairs discourage predators because they irritate the skin and mouth.

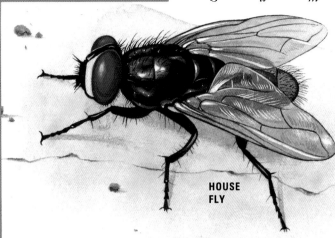

HOUSE FLY

Drone flies have very good eyesight, and their large compound eyes are easily able to spot the movement of an approaching predator. They can be found on flowers on sunny days sucking nectar with their tube-like mouth parts.

DRONE FLY

DIRTY AND DANGEROUS

House flies are common in places where there is food and refuse. They will detect food inside houses, and are attracted to sweet things like jam. They lay their eggs on rotting flesh, and the larvae develop quickly as they eat it. They can spread diseases from animal waste to human food, so should be prevented from landing on it. Like the drone fly, they have good eyes and can detect movements easily.

THE REDSTART HOME

Black redstarts nest in buildings in towns, sometimes using old warehouses and building sites. The nest may be in guttering, or even inside the building. They feed on insects caught on rough ground and sometimes in gardens.

The male black redstart is mostly black with white in the wing; females and juveniles are greyer and less conspicuous. Both have a rusty-red tail. When perched, they sit upright and flick their tails.

BLACK REDSTART

♂ ♀

THE COMMON JACKDAW

The jackdaw is a common bird, regularly seen in towns. It likes to live in a large flock, and its favourite nesting sites are old trees and derelict buildings. Its name derives from its distinctive 'jack-jack' call.

JACKDAW

juv

MAGPIE

Magpies are birds of the countryside which have learnt to live in the town, where they are free from persecution by gamekeepers. They are able to feed by scavenging.

The skies over towns are often filled with insect-catching birds like swifts which nest in buildings and hunt for their food nearby. Swifts are all dark above and have long, narrow wings. They may fly very high, returning to their nests under eaves at dusk.

SWIFT

ROADSIDE BIRD

The kestrel is a familiar bird of roadsides, sometimes seen hovering over grassy verges, or occasionally spotted on a pole or overhead wires, looking down to the ground below for voles, their most important source of food.

Male kestrels have blue-grey heads and tails and are slightly smaller than females. The female has a barred appearance above, and the tail has a number of bands on it. They both hover in one position looking for food, and then make a swift dive to the ground to catch it.

KESTREL

PIGEON NUISANCE

Feral pigeons are common in towns, nesting high up on ledges on buildings. They become quite tame, learning to take food from humans, and quickly spotting scraps and crumbs when people are having their own food. Their droppings can be harmful to old buildings like medieval cathedrals, causing stonework to decay. In some cities, buildings have wire mesh placed over them to keep the pigeons off. Most feral pigeons have two dark bars on the wings and glossy neck patches, but a huge variety of colours will be seen.

FERAL PIGEON

LIKEABLE, LIVELY SPARROWS

House sparrows are the most familiar of all town birds, and are not often seen away from human habitation. They are lively birds, always calling and squabbling with each other and quick to spot a good supply of food on a bird table. They make untidy nests under the eaves of houses and in guttering, using man-made materials like plastic as well as natural products to line nests.

HOUSE SPARROW

75

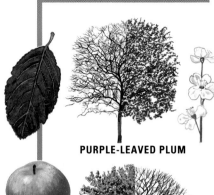

PURPLE-LEAVED PLUM

CULTIVATED APPLE

GUELDER ROSE

COMMON PEAR

The purple-leaved plum is an ornamental tree, often planted in towns for its mass of white blossom in early spring, and its rich copper-coloured leaves which develop later in the summer.

Cultivated apples come in many varieties, and the trees can be large with thick trunks. The blossom is always white or pink with incurved petals.

Guelder rose is a very attractive shrub often found in woods and hedgerows, and occasionally planted in town gardens because of its attractive foliage and shiny red berries.

Common pear may be confused with apple, but the blossom is always white. The pear also grows to be a much taller tree and the bark cracks to form lots of small squares.

YEW

SQUARES AND CHURCHYARDS

The yew is a very slow-growing and long-lived tree, often found in churchyards. It is very poisonous and was once thought to have magical properties. Although it is a type of conifer, it is unusual because its seeds are produced in red, juicy fruits called 'arils'. The London plane earned its name through being very common in central London, where it is very sturdy and resistant to air pollution.

MAKING A RECORD

Carefully but firmly, press some leaves and berries into modelling clay to make a mould. Remove the leaves and berries, make a ring of cardboard around the mould and then pour in plaster of Paris. When it has set, paint the impression of the leaves and berries with enamel paint, matching colours as carefully as you can.

LONDON PLANE

DANDELION

A SEED CLOCK

The familiar 'clock' of the dandelion head occurs in many different habitats. Various seeds will break away from the 'clock' face and scatter on the wind to allow new dandelions to grow where they land.

WILD FLOWERS OF WASTE PLACES

Rosebay willowherb produces large numbers of feathery seeds which are blown by the wind; if any of them settle where there is a scrap of soil, they will grow easily. Great mullein prefers to grow where there is lime in the soil, so the rubble of ruined buildings is very suitable for it. Common chickweed has a very short life-cycle, being able to grow from seed, produce flowers and set new seeds and die in a single year.

ROSEBAY WILLOWHERB

COMMON CHICKWEED

GREAT MULLEIN

STINGING NETTLE

GROUND IVY

COLTSFOOT

FIELD BINDWEED

DAISY

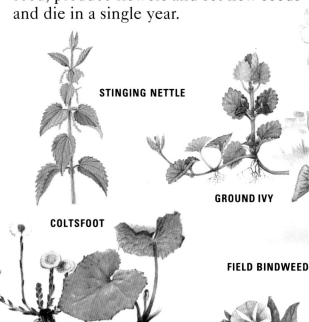

AN ATTRACTIVE CLIMBER

Field bindweed is a nuisance in gardens where it scrambles over other plants and hides them, but in waste places it makes a pleasant splash of colour with its bell-shaped pink and white flowers. It soon covers unsightly fences and posts.

The hawfinch uses its powerful bill, the strongest of any finch, to crack open hard seeds which other birds cannot manage. It usually feeds high in the tree tops, but if a storm blows the seeds down, it may be spotted on the ground. Bramblings also eat seeds and are very fond of beech mast.

Autumn

The fly agaric is a poisonous toadstool found beneath birch trees. It first looks like a white golf ball, but soon splits to reveal the red toadstool beneath.

CHANGING COLOURS

A woodland in autumn is a colourful place as the leaves begin to turn from green to many shades of yellow, red and brown. A few late flowers like golden rod add to the colourful scene. Strange toadstools appear on the woodland floor, and on the trunks of trees, some being hard to spot as they blend in with the fallen leaves. On shrubs, and in the canopy, fruits, nuts and berries ripen and provide food for woodland birds and mammals. Squirrels take the chance to fatten up on seeds and nuts, burying what they can't eat in one go. On mild nights, bats fly for the last time before retreating to their secret winter hibernation sites; they feed on the last of the insects before settling down for the winter when they will have to rely on stored body fat to survive. The male fallow deer lays claim to his favourite clearing in the woods by throwing back his head and making a loud grunting call which carries through the woods, warning the other males to keep away.

Badgers have a busy time in autumn fattening up for the winter. They eat many earthworms and grubs found in the soil, and also search for fruits and berries which help them put on a good layer of fat to keep warm in the winter. They change the bedding of their setts by dragging out all the old material and taking down lots of dry leaves and grass.

Deciduous Woodland

Deciduous trees shed their leaves annually. Because there is such a rich collection of litter from leaves and bark, many species of plants and animals can be found in this type of woodland. The litter provides shelter for mammals, while moths and beetles hide on the woodland floor.

BEECH

EYE-CATCHING DISPLAYS

These trees make very colourful displays in the autumn. The leaves of the beech turn orange, while spindle and wild service tree are covered in beautiful deep red leaves. The fruits are a good guide to recognition: look for the acorns of oaks, the pink-and-orange fruits of spindle and the black clusters of elder berries.

ELDER

NUTS FOR PIGS

Beech nuts are known as 'mast', and can often be found lying on the woodland floor. They are shiny and brown, and contained in a hard, spiny casing. Once the casing has opened, splitting into four sections, the nuts are revealed and then many birds and mammals seek them out. Pigs are especially fond of them, but squirrels and mice also eat as many as they can.

WILD SERVICE TREE

These woodland trees are common throughout Europe. As well as being native in deciduous woods, they are sometimes planted for ornament and, in the case of beech and oak, for their valuable timber.

SPINDLE TREE

FLYING AND FEEDING

Butterflies in woods are usually very active and fast fliers, skimming through the woodland until they stop to rest in the sunlight. When still, the bright colours of the red admiral can be easily seen. In summer and autumn, the chrysalis of this butterfly can be seen suspended from its food plant, and caterpillars are often found wrapped in a nettle leaf. Red admirals prefer to live in sunny, flower-filled places such as woodland clearings, and they will feed on rotting fruit or oozing sap through the autumn.

RED ADMIRAL

As well as the changing colours of leaves in autumn, look out for the bright flash of a red admiral butterfly, or the stunning red of a male bullfinch.

COMMON OAK

BULLFINCH

HAWFINCH

The wood cricket lives amongst the leaf litter of woods, especially under beech trees. Adults can live for up to six months, and most mate and die during autumn or winter.

WOOD CRICKET

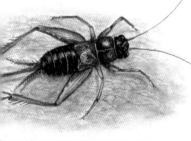

FINCHES AND CREEPERS

These birds live and breed in deciduous woods. The hawfinch and bullfinch both feed on berries, nuts and seeds, and the bill of the hawfinch is extremely large and powerful for this purpose. The beak colour of the male hawfinch changes throughout the year, turning from blue in summer to pale yellow in winter. While the finches feed on the ground and then fly up into the treetops, the treecreeper stays close to the bark of trees, creeping up the trunk with the aid of its long claws, and using its tail as a prop. It may spiral around a tree many times in its search for insects to eat.

TREECREEPER

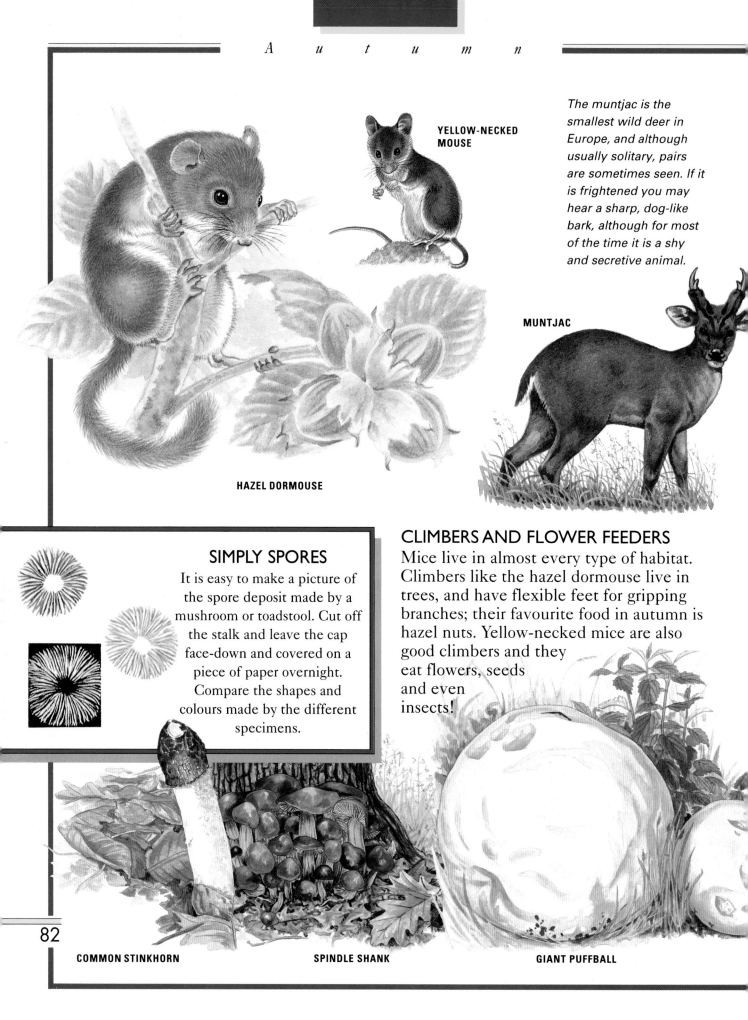

YELLOW-NECKED MOUSE

The muntjac is the smallest wild deer in Europe, and although usually solitary, pairs are sometimes seen. If it is frightened you may hear a sharp, dog-like bark, although for most of the time it is a shy and secretive animal.

MUNTJAC

HAZEL DORMOUSE

SIMPLY SPORES

It is easy to make a picture of the spore deposit made by a mushroom or toadstool. Cut off the stalk and leave the cap face-down and covered on a piece of paper overnight. Compare the shapes and colours made by the different specimens.

CLIMBERS AND FLOWER FEEDERS

Mice live in almost every type of habitat. Climbers like the hazel dormouse live in trees, and have flexible feet for gripping branches; their favourite food in autumn is hazel nuts. Yellow-necked mice are also good climbers and they eat flowers, seeds and even insects!

COMMON STINKHORN   **SPINDLE SHANK**   **GIANT PUFFBALL**

DECEPTIVE DAISIES

Although the two plants shown here do not look very much alike, they both belong to the same plant family - the daisy family - each one having blooms made up of a mass of tiny flowers called florets. They both flower in autumn and produce seeds with fluffy 'parachutes'.

SPEAR THISTLE   **GOLDEN ROD**

FINDING FUNGI

A great variety of fungi grow in woods. They vary in size greatly from small wood mushrooms at only 5cm tall, to the giant puffball which may be over 50cm high - bigger than an adult human head! These fungi will most often be found among the leaf litter of a woodland, or on the roots or bark of deciduous trees.

TAKE-OVER!

The birch polypore shown here is a soft, leathery mushroom which only grows on dead birch trees. It is common, and grows between summer and autumn. Forming a flat brownish cap with white flesh, it looks very much like an open fan. Three are shown growing on the same tree here, but many more can sometimes appear on a single trunk.

BROWN ROLL-RIM   **FLY AGARIC**   **SCALY WOOD MUSHROOM**

83

Coniferous Woodland

The gloomy and silent world of the coniferous woodland becomes lively for a while in autumn as strange and colourful fungi appear on rotting stumps, around tree roots or in the dense carpet of fallen needles. Birds feed on the seeds in the ripening cones, and parasitic insects look for suitable prey before they begin their winter hibernation.

FANTASTIC FUNGI

The dark world of the pine wood is unsuitable for most flowering plants, as they need sunlight. Even in winter, the pine needles block out much of the light, so that the only plants which can grow on the woodland floor are those which need no light. Fungi feed on the remains of other plants or animals, and sometimes attack living trees as well. Many fungi are shaped like a mushroom, with a cap growing on top of a stalk, but some are very strange. The cauliflower fungus grows at the base of trees and appears in the same place each year. The false chanterelle has a funnel-shaped cap, and stands out because of its orange colour, while the purple and yellow plums-and-custard grows in clusters on tree stumps.

PLUMS-AND-CUSTARD

HONEY FUNGUS

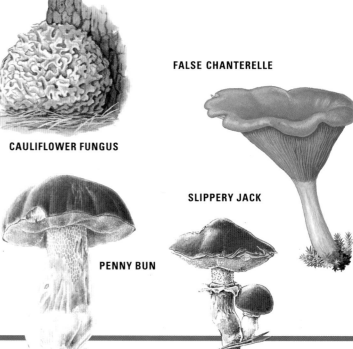

CAULIFLOWER FUNGUS

FALSE CHANTERELLE

SLIPPERY JACK

PENNY BUN

FOOD FOR INSECTS

Most toadstools show signs of being nibbled, and if they are broken open, the flesh of the cap is usually riddled with tiny holes. These are made by the larvae of fungus gnats, fruit flies and tiny beetles. Slugs, snails and millipedes also enjoy eating fungi, and these in turn attract birds which feed on the insects and other creatures. By the time the fungus has completed its development and released its spores, it will have provided food for many woodland creatures.

NATURE'S RECYCLERS

Nothing is wasted in a woodland, not even the discarded pine cones. Although they contain resin and are distasteful to most animals, the *Strobilurus* toadstool can break them down and return the nutrients to the food cycle when it is eaten by insects.

HEDGEHOG FUNGUS

Where many pines grow together, as in man-made plantations, the pine beauty moth can be common. Its green-and-white striped caterpillars are hard to see as they feed on the needles, often causing great damage.

PINE BEAUTY MOTH

NEEDLES AND CONES

The leaves of a pine tree are in the form of needles which grow in bunches; the Scots pine shown here has its needles in bunches of two. They may remain on the tree for two to three years and then fall to the ground to help make a thick, soft carpet. The woody cones are made up of many scales which can open to release seeds or pollen.

BRANCHING FUNGI

Some fungi look nothing like normal toadstools, and can be very hard to identify. Jelly antler fungus grows in tufts on rotting stumps of conifers, and has rounded, antler-shaped stems with a jelly-like feel. Meadow coral is very similar, but grows out of the soil in grassland and woodland clearings, and has slightly flattened stems.

SCOTS PINE

JELLY ANTLER   **MEADOW CORAL**

85

SEED EATERS

Coniferous woodlands provide a feast of seeds for the birds who can find them. The tough cones of pines have many seeds protected by tough, woody scales; these open in damp weather, but for much of the time they remain closed, so birds must be able to extract the seeds from between the scales. The curious bill of the crossbill is ideally suited to getting between the scales; they are prised open by the bill, and the tongue is used to extract the seeds. After feeding, the cone is dropped from the tree by the bird.

SISKIN

REDPOLL

CROSSBILL

CRESTED TIT

Pine woods often have other tree species such as birch and alder growing in them, and these provide food for smaller seed-eating finches like the siskin and redpoll. These birds often feed in excitable mixed flocks, and will move from place to place in their search for food.

AN AGILE FEEDER

The small crested tit sometimes gives away its position by its purring call; if seen, its black and white crest helps identify it. This tiny bird is able to perch at the ends of twigs and search for food amongst the needles of conifers and the buds of broad-leaved trees. In the breeding season it keeps to its own territory, but in autumn it will join with other small woodland birds to form mixed feeding flocks.

NESTING

Crested tits make their nests in rotten tree stumps, preferably a pine, but they will sometimes use other trees or even old wooden posts. They easily excavate their own nests, pecking away at the rotten wood with their sharp bills and creating a pile of woodchippings at the base of the stump. The pair will defend their nesting site aggressively, driving away any other birds who show an interest.

PINE HAWK MOTH

The large pine hawk moth can be one of the most difficult to find as its excellent camouflage helps it to match exactly the bark of pine trees, where it rests during the day. It only leaves its hiding place at night to fly in search of somewhere to lay eggs. The caterpillars resemble the pine needles they feed on, and the chrysalis is buried in the soil at the base of the tree.

WASP TAKE-OVER

Ichneumon wasps lay their eggs directly inside the bodies of other insects, usually the caterpillars of moths and butterflies. The eggs hatch into tiny larvae which eat their host's body from the inside, not killing it straight away, but keeping it alive to act as a food store. Cocoons on the outside of a caterpillar show that it has been attacked.

ROWAN

ICHNEUMON WASP

Both the wood wasp and ichneumon wasp are fast-flying, and constantly in motion through a pine wood. They can be identified by their long ovipostors, protruding from the back of the abdomen.

WOOD WASP OR HORNTAIL

WOOD WASPS

The frightening-looking wood wasp, or horntail, has the colourings of the more familiar common wasps, and a formidable-looking 'sting' at the end of its abdomen, but it is harmless to humans. Its 'sting' is the ovipostor used by females to insert their eggs into the trunks of pine trees. The eggs hatch into larvae which may take up to three years to develop as they eat the tough tissues of the pine tree. They may be parasitised by ichneumon wasps during this time.

Park & Garden

Gardens put on one last show of colour in the autumn before winter sets in. Sunny days encourage butterflies to feed on the many nectar-producing plants still in flower before they look for a sheltered place to hibernate. Damp weather brings on a display of curious fungi, some growing in rings on lawns, and others appearing on stumps, or even gravel paths.

SUN AND COLOUR

When the sun shines, butterflies flock to their favourite garden plants, which release sugary nectar, giving them the energy needed to cope with flying, egg-laying and even a long winter hiberna-tion. Peacocks flick their brightly-marked wings, revealing large eye-spots, while gatekeepers sit more sedately on the flowers showing off orange and brown patches, and a flash of blue indicates that the holly blue is not far away. Painted ladies may be long distance migrants, having travelled over land and sea to reach northern breeding grounds.

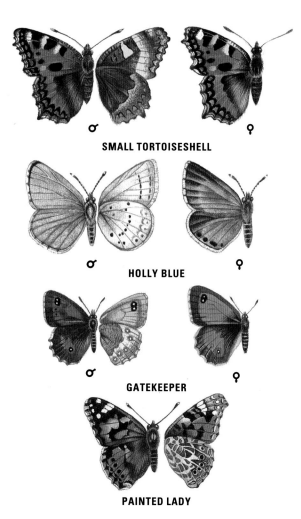

SMALL TORTOISESHELL

HOLLY BLUE

GATEKEEPER

PAINTED LADY

PEACOCK

WING PATTERNS

Other butterflies and predators, like small birds, cannot mistake the striking wing pattern of the peacock, which acts as an excellent warning. When its wings are folded, the dark underside makes it look like a dead leaf, providing superb camouflage for its winter hibernation.

CANDLE SNUFF FUNGUS

CANDLE SNUFF

Long after a tree has been cut down and the stump has begun to rot away, small branching black-and-white stems of candle snuff will grow out of it, often after a spell of cold weather. This tiny fungus releases clouds of white spores whenever an animal brushes past it.

AUTUMN FUNGI

However tidy a gardener may be, there will always be the remains of dead plants, grass clippings, fallen leaves and other organic matter lying around the garden, and all of these materials will be food for fungi, just as they are in woodland. Many of these fungi are the gardener's friends, as they help to tidy the garden by removing unwanted waste, and returning the nutrients to the soil, but some will be pests, because they can attack living plants as well, or disfigure lawns and flower borders.

ORANGE PEEL FUNGUS

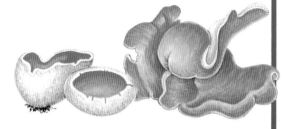

The buried remains of plants, old twigs, and even grass clippings provide food for the orange peel fungus which will even grow on paths as long as there is some food buried below it.

FAIRY RING CHAMPIGNON

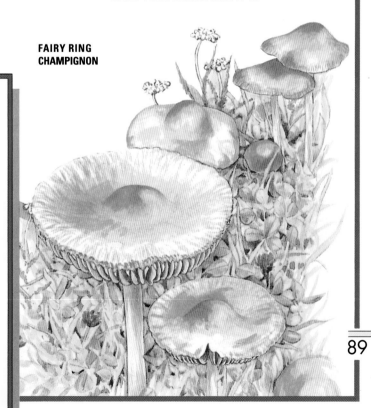

FAIRY RINGS

Mysterious dark green rings of thick grass in the lawn will suddenly produce a crop of small toadstools in autumn. The tiny fairy ring champignon toadstools grow in a ring formation. The toadstools remove food matter from the centre of the ring, so new toadstools must grow on the outside, increasing the size of the ring every year.

89

BLACKBIRD

MISTLE THRUSH

REDWING

FIELDFARE

A FEAST OF BERRIES

Autumn can be a time of plenty for birds in parks and gardens as so many berry-bearing trees and shrubs will be producing food. The thrush family are especially fond of berries, and will feed all day on their favourite fruits.

HUNGRY MIGRANTS

Fieldfares and redwings, members of the thrush family which breed in northern areas, move south before the winter sets in to escape from harsh weather and find a reliable food supply. They are attracted to berry-bearing trees and shrubs, but have to compete with the resident blackbirds and mistle thrushes who are already guarding them. When they have eaten all the berries they can find in woods and hedgerows, they move into towns.

NERVOUS MOORHENS

Moorhens are nervous birds, but they can overcome their fear of humans if there is a good supply of food to tempt them. Ponds and lakes in town parks are often busy places, and moorhens have learnt to take scraps intended for other birds like ducks, and will venture further and further away from the water when they are really hungry.

MOORHEN

juv

BATHING BLACKBIRD

Blackbirds like to bathe in water to clear any unwelcome creatures out of their feathers. They are very clean birds, and need to do this cleaning exercise to ensure that nothing slows them down in flight, or ruins the insulation their feathers provide.

TREES FROM AROUND THE WORLD

Many elegant and attractive trees from around the world have found their way into parks and gardens. Their stately appearance, beautiful flowers and foliage, and interesting fruits and seeds have attracted the attention of gardeners who have planted and cared for these trees. They also benefit the wildlife, especially the birds, living in these gardens, as they provide food, shelter from harsh weather and secure nesting sites. Evergreen trees are popular because they provide colour and shelter throughout the year.

FRAGRANT CEDARS

The stately cedar trees are often planted in gardens because of their interesting shapes, but they also have scented foliage and fragrant wood. Some produce cones like large wooden eggs. Young cones appear in spring at the tips of stems; male cones drop off, but female cones remain and grow.

All of the trees shown on this page are evergreen conifers. Their green foliage will brighten up the dullest park or garden in the winter.

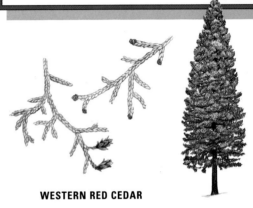

WESTERN RED CEDAR

LEYLAND CYPRESS

CEDAR OF LEBANON

91

Town

Town gardens attract many insects, spiders, slugs and snails, and some gardeners worry about what harm they might do to their plants, but many of these small creatures are harmless, and some are even very helpful. If left alone, the helpful insects will pollinate flowers, remove waste, destroy pests and make the garden a more interesting place to be in.

WHITE-TAILED BUMBLE BEE

The long tongue of the bumble bee helps it to reach inside flowers to find nectar, and its hairy body picks up pollen grains which it carries from flower to flower.

HONEY BEE

BUSY BEES

As honey bees fly from flower to flower collecting nectar to make honey, they also carry pollen and help to pollinate fruit trees, garden crops like peas and beans, soft fruits such as strawberries, and many garden flowers, so without the bees few seeds would form. In the autumn a rich harvest of honey is provided to be shared by the bees and the beekeeper

The elegant lacewing fly has delicately-veined wings and bright metallic-looking eyes. It seeks out small insect prey like greenfly, but in autumn looks for a secure, dry place to hibernate, often a shed or greenhouse.

GREEN LACEWING

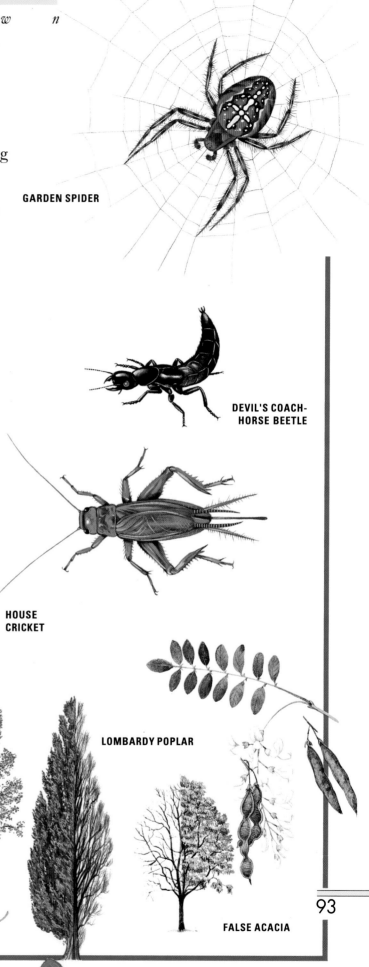

GARDEN SPIDER

PREDATOR AND PREY

On misty autumn mornings, drops of dew highlight the cobwebs spun during the night by garden spiders. These beautifully-patterned webs are constructed to catch flying insects, and trap them as food for the spider. Scurrying through the undergrowth is the strange devil's coach-horse, a wingless beetle able to eject a stream of foul-smelling liquid at predators from its upturned tail. Garden snails find plenty to eat in autumn, and their silvery trails on paths in the morning show where they fed the night before. House crickets are nocturnal creatures, so look out for them at night.

GARDEN SNAIL

DEVIL'S COACH-HORSE BEETLE

HOUSE CRICKET

AUTUMN TREES

The seed pods of the false acacia become dry and brittle in autumn, and its seeds can then be dispersed. The ridged bark sometimes has thorny sprouts emerging from it. Lombardy poplars are trees which prefer marshy ground and need plenty of water. When planted in towns, they soak up so much water from the soil that the soil can shrink and damage the foundations of buildings.

LOMBARDY POPLAR

The balm of Gilead is a popular town park tree with clusters of attractive, multi-coloured leaves and reddish-brown stems; it also has a slight fragrance. Like other poplars, it should be planted in damp places as its roots take up large volumes of water.

BALM OF GILEAD

FALSE ACACIA

ARRIVALS AND DEPARTURES

Autumn is the season when many of the familiar birds of summer depart for warmer climates; their supplies of insect food will have dwindled, and they will need to move south, often covering vast distances, to spend the winter in a warmer place where insects are plentiful.

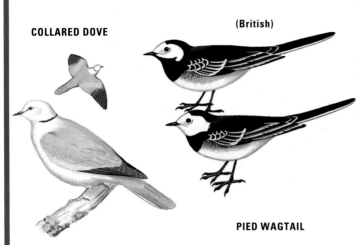

COLLARED DOVE

(British)

PIED WAGTAIL

HOUSE MARTIN

LONG-DISTANCE MIGRANTS

The length and duration of the journeys undertaken by some small birds are quite staggering; they cover whole continents as the tiny birds leave harsh northern winters and head for better feeding conditions further south. Where possible, birds avoid flying over water, taking long detours overland to reach ocean-crossing places which are the shortest. Often, large numbers of migrants congregate at important crossing places like the Strait of Gibraltar or Panama. Each spring, there is a return migration along the same routes as birds return to their breeding grounds.

House martins may congregate on overhead wires and rooftops, then feed together in huge flocks, before finally departing. The map below shows the migration routes for both martins and swallows.

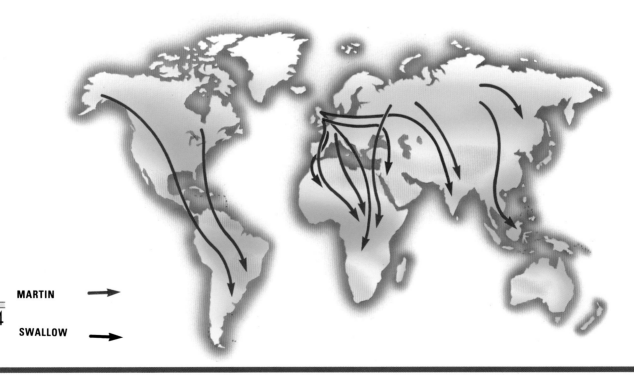

MARTIN →

SWALLOW →

SHEPHERD'S PURSE

GROUNDSEL

WHITE DEAD-NETTLE

FLOWERS AND SEEDS

A few familiar garden weeds are able to continue flowering and setting seed as long as fine weather lasts in autumn. Shepherd's purse thrives in the disturbed ground of gardens, and its seeds can germinate in quite cold conditions. When groundsel produces its familiar fluffy seed heads in autumn, these attract feeding birds like goldfinches. White dead-nettle produces flowers which attract bees anxious for a last feed of nectar.

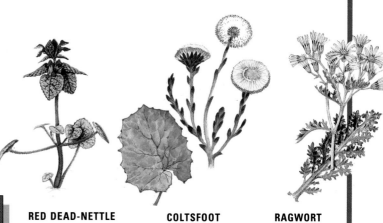

RED DEAD-NETTLE   **COLTSFOOT**   **RAGWORT**

POPULAR FLOWERS

Insects are still busy on sunny days in autumn, so the few flowers that remain receive many visitors. Honey bees, bumble bees, and some late hoverflies will be attracted to any supply of nectar. Wasps are especially attracted to the clustered yellow flowers of ivy.

LATE AUTUMN COLOURS

There is still some colour in the last days of autumn, especially in sheltered places like gardens. When the more showy garden flowers die back, smaller plants like the dead-nettles get a chance to reach the light and attract pollinating insects. Poisonous ragwort produces its white, parachute-like seeds on its brown, withered, flower stalks, while, below, next year's rosettes of leaves look green and healthy. The seeds of coltsfoot will have dispersed long ago, but the large grey-green leaves will persist until killed by the first frosts.

95

The Strand Line

Autumn gales throw the remains of the summer's growth of seaweeds on to the shore, and this collects on the strand line, just above the high tide mark, to provide food and shelter for many scavengers. Grey seals produce their pups in autumn, and until they can fend for themselves, the pups will live on the shore.

GREY SEAL

COMMON SEAL

MONK SEAL

GREY SEAL

The grey seal's large nose and spotted markings help identify it, even if only the head is seen. The common seal has a more rounded head and shorter nose, with V-shaped nostrils, while the rare monk seal is all brown, with a white patch on its underside.

LARGE AND SMALL

Some of our largest, and also some of the smallest mammals, can be found on the strand line at times. The huge grey seal, about 3m long, comes ashore to produce its pups in autumn. The smaller common seal produces its pups earlier in the year, but also likes to haul itself out on sandy beaches. The very rare monk seal lives only in the Mediterranean and comes ashore on the most deserted beaches in autumn to produce its dark-furred pups. The tiny pygmy shrew is only 6cm long, and the lesser white-toothed shrew reaches only 7cm, but these minute mammals are enthusiastic feeders on sandhoppers, sea slaters and insects found in rotting seaweeds.

PYGMY SHREW

LESSER WHITE-TOOTHED SHREW

TANGLEWEED OR OARWEED

All through the summer the large oarweeds will have been growing larger and larger, but in autumn the thick growth is torn away by gales and cast ashore. Many tiny creatures live on the oarweed, and these will be cast ashore too, to be eaten by birds and shrews.

TANGLEWEED OR OARWEED

THONGWEED

FURBELOWS

SEA BOOTLACE OR MERMAID'S FISHING LINES

SEA OAK OR PODWEED

SUGAR KELP OR POOR MAN'S WEATHER GLASS

THE UNDERWATER FOREST

Below the low water mark, where the tide never retreats, is an underwater forest of colourful seaweeds which grow both longer and larger through the summer. Each one is fixed to the rocks by a tough, sticky 'hand' called a holdfast. The top growth releases spores into the water, which eventually form new seaweeds, but each autumn this growth is torn off and swept to the shore where it forms large deposits; as it rots, it is eaten by kelp fly larvae, sea slaters and sand-hoppers, and these in turn are eaten by other creatures.

SCAVENGERS

If a piece of seaweed or driftwood is lifted up, sea slaters, looking like giant woodlice, will scurry away. These common scavengers live just above the high tide line. Their favourite food is pieces of rotting seaweed, and they are most active at night, emerging from their hiding places to feed in the open.

A USEFUL SEAWEED

The sugar kelp was once used to feed people, as it could be boiled to make a form of soup. Its other name of 'weather glass' reminds us of how it was once used to foretell rain; in the damp air before a rainstorm it would absorb moisture and feel sticky, but in dry weather it would feel dry and brittle.

97

MARRAM GRASS

BUILDING THE COASTLINE

One of the most important plants on the seashore is marram grass. Its wiry stems and leaves help it to survive the windblown sand and salt spray common in exposed places, but more importantly, its vast root system holds it firm in the sand and holds the sand in place as well. Without its binding roots the sand would soon blow away, and many other more delicate plants would suffer in stormy weather. In many places, marram grass is planted in order to protect the coastline.

SEA ROCKET

FLOATING SEEDS

Several colourful plants grow on the strand line, and keep flowering until autumn. They produce floating seeds, so when the high tides of autumn wash around their roots, the seeds can be carried away to find new parts of the shore to grow on. Sea kale produces large numbers of seeds in rounded woody pods, and sea sandwort produces shiny yellow capsules which contain small salt-water resistant seeds.

SEA SANDWORT

SEA BINDWEED

Sea rocket grows on the strand line as close as it can to the sea. Its seed pods contain many floating seeds, which may be blown inland by the wind, but may also be carried to a suitable beach by the sea. Sea bindweed twines its stems around the marram grass, its shiny, rounded leaves contrasting strongly with the wiry leaves of the marram grass.

SEA KALE

2 years old

HERRING GULL

GREAT BLACK-BACKED GULL

2 years old

LESSER BLACK-BACKED GULL

LOOKING FOR FOOD

After a busy breeding season, gulls disperse around the coastline in search of food. The largest is the great black-backed, with its all-black wings, which may not travel far from its breeding site. The lesser black-backed gull, with its slaty-grey wings with black tips, may travel far inland to rubbish dumps, or even make a long migration along the coast to a much warmer climate for winter. The herring gull has silvery-grey wings with dark tips, and it also travels far in search of food, sometimes visiting rubbish dumps and reservoirs.

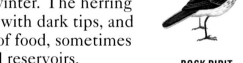

ROCK PIPIT

COMMON NECKLACE SHELL

A NECKLACE OF EGGS

The necklace shell earned its name through producing a necklace-like band of eggs; as it lays its eggs on sandy beaches, it binds them up in a mixture of sand and mucus to form a long curved ribbon. This mollusc makes a curved path through the sand as it moves.

The necklace shell is a predator attacking other sand-dwelling molluscs; it furrows through the sand searching for tiny cockles, and then drills through their shells with its tongue and sucks out the contents, leaving empty shells with tiny holes in them.

ROCK PIPIT

The rock pipit breeds in holes in rocky sea cliffs, but in winter moves on to the strand line, where it finds a plentiful supply of insects amongst rotting seaweeds. Its sharp eyes help it spot the movements of kelp flies, and its quick movements make it a skilled hunter of small insects. It may also utter its shrill 'tseep-it' call from time to time.

The fox has learnt that a garden makes a good hunting place. House mice live here and can be stalked among garden plants and shrubs. The fox will have to learn to compete with a cat or dog which may also live in the garden. They often come to take food put out for them by people, and soon become used to the lights of the house.

Winter

The bright red berries of holly are an attraction to birds like thrushes, and many are eaten when the weather becomes harsh.

A WINTER WONDERLAND

A garden in winter is a good place for watching wildlife because birds and mammals can be attracted close to the house by offering them food. If a bird table is placed close to a window, the birds can be watched in comfort. In very cold weather the birds will appreciate offerings of food, especially sunflower seeds and peanuts, fat and clean drinking water. A good wildlife garden will also have plenty of natural food in the form of wild seeds and berries left behind by a considerate gardener. A few apples left on the tree, and the dried heads of teasels and burdock, will help attract thrushes and finches. The tawny owl sometimes roosts in old trees in gardens, and its pellets may be found on the ground beneath its favourite perch. Some birds, such as starlings, will fly from the countryside into a town at night to roost on buildings, since towns are usually more sheltered places than the open countryside, and are so much warmer.

Many creatures hibernate in the garden, finding safe hiding places in compost heaps, beneath flower pots or under ivy. Hedgehogs make a thick nest of leaves, and roll themselves into a tight ball inside it. Garden snails attach themselves to stones or crawl into the base of shrubs, and the bright yellow brimstone butterfly hides beneath dead leaves.

Deciduous Woodland

During cold winter weather, many animals sleep soundly in secret nests, unaware of what is happening around them. Some, like deer, must continue to search for food, even in the harshest weather. Birds roost in the shelter of woodlands at night, and make forays out into the countryside during the day to search for food.

STINKING HELLEBORE

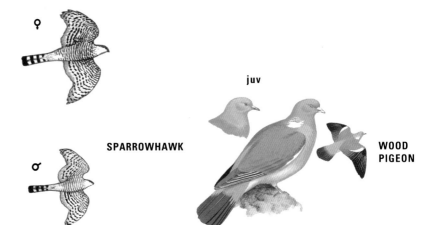

♀

juv

SPARROWHAWK

♂

WOOD PIGEON

HARDY FLOWERS

While there is no activity for most flowers in winter, a few hardy species manage to keep their green leaves, and even produce flowers. On mild days, when a little sunshine reaches the woodland floor, they open and may attract a few pollinating insects. The stinking hellebore earns its name by having strong-smelling leaves and flowers; its tough leaves withstand frost and snow.

FINDING FOOD

The wood pigeon is clever at finding food in winter, despite harsh conditions. Large flocks of pigeons roost in woodlands at night, and then fly out in all directions in search of food in fields and gardens. When some find food, many others will spot them feeding and fly down to join them: soon, a huge flock gathers. At night they return to the safety of the woods to roost.

The sparrowhawk lurks in a concealed place in the woods waiting for a small bird to fly past. As soon as it does, the sparrowhawk can capture it with its long talons.

HEDGEHOG

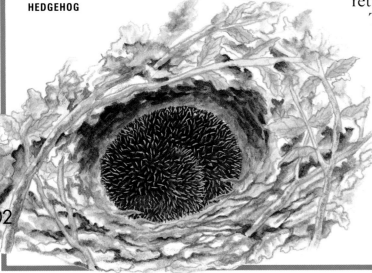

The male roe deer keeps its antlers for a short time in winter, but soon sheds them, whilst the larger male sika deer keeps its antlers until the spring. Both deer take on a darker colouration in winter, and a thicker coat to help them survive in harsh weather; they spend much time feeding in thickets and dense cover.

ROE DEER

SIKA DEER

THE LONG SLEEP

For many small mammals, winter is a very difficult time; there is very little of their favourite food to be found, and they are unable to keep themselves warm in cold weather. The best thing to do is sleep soundly in a secret hiding place until warm weather returns in the spring. Hedgehogs make a leafy nest under logs or bushes, and then hide in it for several months. Hibernating mammals lower their body temperatures to just above air temperature and slow down their breathing and heartbeat rates; in this way they use very little energy and can survive on stored fat reserves for many weeks. The grey squirrel will curl up in its home, called a drey, to keep warm in the winter months. However, it will not hibernate, as it can only survive for a few days without food.

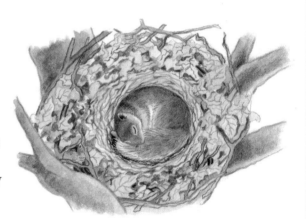

GREY SQUIRREL

UNROLLING HEDGEHOG

VELVET SHANK

HAIRY LEATHER-BRACKET

THE SURVIVORS!

Many fungi are killed by frost, but a few tough species survive through the winter. Many of these are leathery bracket fungi which grow out of tree trunks and branches, and may persist for several years. Both the hairy leather-bracket and the blushing bracket form thick lobes which stand out on dead wood, whilst the artist's fungus forms more fleshy lobes nearer the base of a tree. The brightly-coloured cup fungi are conspicuous on the woodland floor in winter, growing on fallen twigs and leaves and often reappearing in the same place year after year. Some winter fungi, like the wood warts, are smaller and harder to find; these must be searched for on fallen twigs and rotting logs. The brightly-coloured velvet shank can tolerate being frozen solid, and when it thaws it starts producing spores again.

RED WOOD-WART

SCARLET ELF-CUP

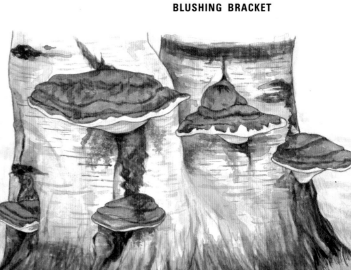

BLUSHING BRACKET

ARTIST'S FUNGUS

YELLOW-MILK CUP

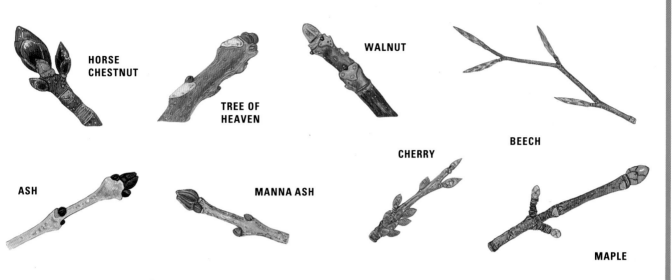

HORSE CHESTNUT

TREE OF HEAVEN

WALNUT

BEECH

CHERRY

ASH

MANNA ASH

MAPLE

SWEET CHESTNUT

HORNBEAM

READING THE TREES

Trees can easily be recognized in winter by the appearance of twigs and buds. Some are very striking, like the fat sticky buds of horse chestnut, the sharply-pointed buds of beech, or the sooty-black buds of ash. Others can be recognized by the way their buds are arranged in clusters at the tips of the twigs, like this oak. Make a collection of the twigs of trees in your area, and arrange them on a card with labels beside them.

TREE SPOTTING

Some trees stand out in winter as they keep all their leaves and have a crop of bright berries as well. Holly is a well known tree, but is more common than people think. During the summer it is hidden by deciduous trees; in winter when they have lost their leaves it stands out well. Winter is the best time to search for holly. Look for the 'browse line' on the lower branches showing where hungry deer have nibbled the leaves.

HOLLY

105

Coniferous Woodland

The silent world of the coniferous forest is not completely deserted in winter. Tiny goldcrests and wrens search for insects amongst the pine needles, while the goshawk and long-eared owl seek larger prey.

GOLDCREST

WREN

GOSHAWK

LONG-EARED OWL

SPOTTED!

The tiny goldcrest inhabits the tree canopy of the coniferous forest and, although it is very small, it can be spotted by looking carefully at the tips of the branches where it searches for insects. Its thin, scratchy call will also give a clue to its position.

EATING AND SCOLDING

The goldcrest seeks its food in the tree canopy, but the wren, which is only a little larger, searches amongst fallen branches and in the undergrowth for its insect food. Its scolding calls, and surprisingly loud song, are tell-tale clues to its whereabouts. Several scolding wrens may mean there is a long-eared owl nearby - they will mob it if they find one! They will also make their alarm calls if the goshawk flies by.

A TREE FOR CHRISTMAS

The Norway spruce is the familiar Christmas tree, harvested in thousands in winter to decorate homes for Christmas. Its tough, spiky needles have a woody stump at the base, so when they fall off they leave a scar on the twig. The tree has a particular scent which is strongest in damaged twigs and leaves. Mature trees produce long, smooth, flexible cones which hang downwards from the branches and can often be found on the ground beneath the tree. The cones can be bent in your hands without breaking.

NORWAY SPRUCE

The herald of the winter is a common fungus of conifer woods, and usually waits for the first frosts before putting in an appearance. It grows in small groups on the woodland floor, its brown cap making it difficult to spot against a carpet of pine needles.

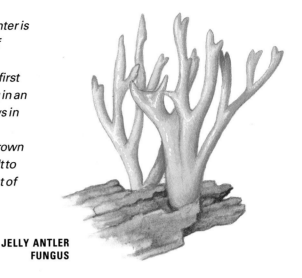

JELLY ANTLER FUNGUS

HERALD OF THE WINTER

The bright yellow branching stems of the jelly antler fungus stand out against the dark background of the dead conifer stumps they usually grow on.

WINTER FUNGI

The accumulation of needles, cones, twigs and debris on the woodland floor provides a constant supply of food for many species of fungi. Nothing is wasted, and even in mid-winter many colourful toadstools occur. The violet conifer bracket is especially common where trees have been damaged by fire, but it is also frequently found on fallen conifer trunks. It sometimes forms tiers of brackets with violet-tinged wavy margins. Look closely at the fungi for signs of feeding slugs, and the burrowings of insect larvae.

VIOLET CONIFER BRACKET

EAR PICK FUNGUS

Fallen and partly buried pine cones are often colonized by small groups of the curious ear pick fungus, which is easily recognized by its kidney-shaped cap and hairy appearance.

107

PINE MARTEN

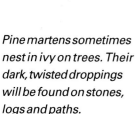

Pine martens sometimes nest in ivy on trees. Their dark, twisted droppings will be found on stones, logs and paths.

RED SQUIRREL

AN AGILE CLIMBER

The pine marten is a very nimble predator, easily able to pursue other mammals through the trees and over the ground. Its claws help it grip on to bark, and its long tail is used for balance. Good eyesight, excellent hearing and a keen sense of smell help the marten locate its prey. It will chase red squirrels and birds through the tree tops. The pine marten spends much of its day sleeping quietly in a favourite resting place, preferring to hunt at night. If spotted by small birds, they will mob it furiously until it moves off. Martens will eat fruits and berries at times, especially if animal food is hard to find.

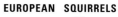
EUROPEAN SQUIRRELS

The red squirrel is a seed-eater which gnaws away at the scales of pine cones to get the seeds, leaving the central stalk of the cone on a stump.

ARCTIC FOX

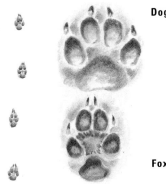

Dog

Fox

Reindeer live wild in the remotest parts of northern Europe, making long migrations in search of food.

REINDEER

FEET AND ANTLERS

Reindeer have very large feet to cope with walking in soft snow. Their rounded feet leave curved 'slots' or tracks. The large antlers are flattened at the tips and also have a forward-pointing section with many points and flattened lobes. Both males and females have antlers, but the female's are smaller.

TRACKS AND SIGNS OF WINTER MAMMALS

The arctic fox moults from its summer brown fur into a thick white coat in winter, and has an especially bushy tail to help keep it warm while it is sleeping. It leaves neat tracks in the snow; its rounded pads show clearly, and often there are impressions of the claws and hair as well. Foxes always walk in a straight line with one print exactly behind the next one, but dogs seem to be walking sideways, with their larger, broader prints appearing to be more spread out. Fox droppings are often left near the site of a kill, so there may be signs of a struggle, or some fur or feathers lying on the ground nearby.

Mountain

Winter conditions on mountains can be very harsh, and only the most hardy of birds and mammals can survive there; many of them change their appearance to match the snow-covered landscape. A few trees grow on mountains, becoming more stunted nearer the high mountain tops. Exposed rocks are often covered with colourful displays of lichens.

MOUNTAIN BIRDS

The majestic golden eagle soars over mountains in winter in search of prey. It may take mammals like the mountain hare, feed on larger animals which have died from the cold, or pursue the ptarmigan, a resident bird of high mountains, still present in winter. The all-black raven will search for dead animals, and may also feed on the remains of an eagle's kill. Tiny snow buntings peck around on the ground for grass seeds and other scraps, only leaving the high mountain tops in the most severe weather.

GOLDEN EAGLE

RAVEN

SNOW BUNTING

σ

♀

In winter the ptarmigan is almost all white, with feathers covering its feet and legs. It shows dark patches on its tail when it is in flight.

Summer

Winter

PTARMIGAN

MOUNTAIN PINE

COMMON SILVER FIR

The mountain pine's stiff, dense needles grow in a spiral-like way around the shoots. Its greyish bark can be almost black at times. The silver fir is a much larger tree with more dense branches. Its needles have two white bands on the underside.

SNOWY FLOWERS

Some mountain flowers, such as the alpine snowbell, begin to bloom before the winter snows have melted away.

Their flowers push up through the snow into the sunlight while the leaves remain covered up below. As the snow melts, the flowers wither and the leaves are exposed. The blanket of snow protects the leaves and the roots of the snowbell from icy winds and much colder weather.

TOUGH TREES

Heavy winter snowfall can damage trees as it builds up on the branches, so mountain trees are especially adapted to cope with this. Most trees on high mountains are conifers. Their conical shape allows snow to slip down the tree from branch to branch and the needles are fine enough to prevent each one from holding very much snow. Many mountain trees are strong enough to resist high winds, and they can also tolerate very low temperatures for long periods. They are mostly slow-growing but can live for many years.

Bright yellow-green patches of lichen on exposed rocks, with a pattern of black lines and dots, reveal the striking mountain lichen. It is sometimes known as map lichen because of its similarity to countries shaded in on the page of an atlas.

MOUNTAIN LICHEN

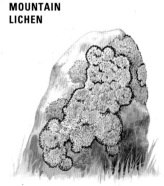

THE NERVOUS CHAMOIS

The chamois grows a thick, dark brown coat in winter. When challenging another chamois, it can raise the hair on its back, making it look very rough-coated. The curved horns point backwards, and are used by males to fight and butt each other in late autumn and winter. Chamois must be approached carefully from a downwind direction in order to be observed, as they are very nervous of humans. This is an endangered mammal as a result of persecution and disturbance by winter sports.

CHAMOIS

MOUFLON

SURE-FOOTED ANIMALS

Mountain-dwelling mammals like the mouflon and chamois are very sure-footed on rocky ground, and are easily able to flee from predators on steep slopes, or search for food in dangerous places. They browse on trees and shrubs, but also feed on grasses, sedges and lichens. Males compete with each other for small herds of females during the rutting season, usually late autumn. Males happily graze together in groups until the rut, then they start to fight.

RED DEER

In winter, the red deer loses the foxy-red coat which gives it its name and grows a thicker grey-brown coat for extra warmth. Many males sport splendid antlers, with several points, or tines, on each side. Females lack the antlers and are slightly smaller than the males. After the autumn rut, the males and females will search for food on high ground, unless driven down from the hills by harsh weather. They are very wary of humans, and can only be observed at close range if approached quietly from downwind. Each herd will have a few look-outs ready to warn the rest of the herd of danger.

RED DEER

ALPINE MARMOT

Marmots hibernate in a nest at the end of a deep burrow and will not emerge during snow, but they may feed on food they have stored underground.

WHITE-COATED HARE

The mountain, or blue hare, grows a white coat in winter. If it does this before the winter snows fall, it is very conspicuous. Its ears are shorter than those of the brown hare, but they still have the characteristic black tips.

MOUNTAIN PREDATORS

Predators must continue to hunt during winter, but they may have to endure short periods without food when the weather is too severe to hunt. Because of centuries of persecution by man, many of these predators are now only found in remote areas such as mountains. The secretive lynx hunts mainly at night, and is rarely seen. The wildcat is also very difficult to observe, spending most of the day in hiding, and emerging to feed on small mammals and birds only at night.

The wildcat's tail is much thicker than the domestic cat's, and blunt at the tip with striking ring-markings.

Wildcat tail

Domestic cat tail

LYNX

The wildcat looks similar to an overgrown tabby cat, but it is wilder and much more fierce. Both the lynx and the wildcat are secretive woodland animals and the wildcat is a very agile climber. The short tail and tufted ears make the lynx quite distinctive. The lynx is not found in the United Kingdom.

WILDCAT

113

Estuary

The bleak expanse of an estuary in winter may seem to be very uninviting, but many plants and animals can be found there. Some birds will have travelled vast distances from even more harsh conditions to make use of the rich food supplies available in the sand and mud.

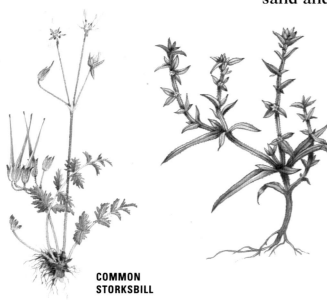

PRICKLY SALTWORT

COMMON STORKSBILL

FLOWERING PLANTS

Few plants can survive winter conditions on the shores of an estuary, but some thrive in the open sandy conditions on the shoreline. Common storksbill is a flower whose leaf rosette is commonly seen in bare sandy places. Prickly saltwort is very tolerant of salt water, growing close to the high-tide line, and is sometimes completely washed over by the waves. It has tough prickly stems and leaves for protection.

SIPHONING FOOD

The very common peppery furrow shell lives buried in the sand unless washed out by a storm. It extends two thin siphons to the surface to feed on tiny food particles. If a few specimens are placed in a shady container of sea water, they will extend their siphons after a few minutes. Huge numbers of empty shells will be found along the shores of estuaries after winter gales; gulls will feed greedily on the living molluscs when they are first dislodged from the sand.

PEPPERY FURROW SHELL

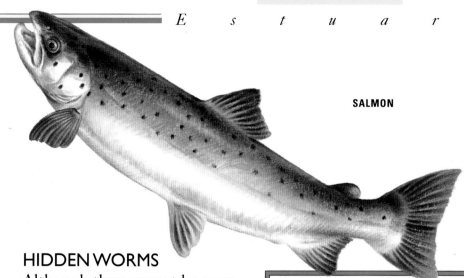

SALMON

Salmon leave their feeding grounds far out to sea, and swim through estuaries to their spawning sites in freshwater rivers. They need to spend some time in the estuary adjusting to the change from sea water to fresh water.

HIDDEN WORMS

Although they cannot be seen, there are vast numbers of different species of worms living buried in the mud of estuaries. They feed on small particles of food in the mud or on its surface. Most of them make burrows, and they remain in these at low tide, safe from predators. When the tide returns, some will emerge to feed and may then be caught by fish or wading birds for whom they are a very important food.

JUMPING SALMON

Salmon always move through estuaries at the same time each year, although for different estuaries these times may be different. They usually wait for heavy rain to fall inland before making their way upstream by jumping weirs and waterfalls. Find out from local fishermen when the salmon run, and then watch at weirs and bridges at the head of the estuary for migrating salmon.

RAGWORM

RAGGED WORMS

The ragworm is a colourful worm, with a frilled edge to the body. It uses these frills to help swim when it leaves its burrow. Its head is armed with sharp jaws for seizing its prey, and it is itself a favourite food of many fish.

LUGWORM

The lugworm is a favourite fishing bait for sea anglers, and large numbers are dug out of the sand every day. Lugworms live in a U-shaped burrow and leave a worm-like cast of sand near to one of the holes.

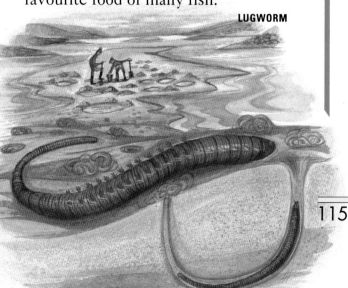

115

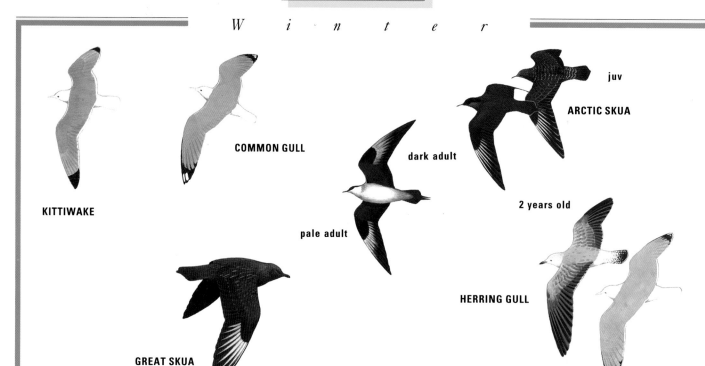

KITTIWAKE

COMMON GULL

juv

ARCTIC SKUA

dark adult

pale adult

2 years old

HERRING GULL

GREAT SKUA

light-breasted

dark-breasted   BRENT GOOSE

♀

♂

SHELDUCK

A FEAST FOR WADING BIRDS

Enormous numbers of birds converge on estuaries in the winter. Some of these will be wildfowl and gulls, others will be waders, and some will be specialized feeders like the grey heron. Scavenging gulls are always present, but for a time they may be pursued by predatory skuas, on their way to their southern wintering areas. Brent geese come together in flocks of thousands, feeding on eel grass and green algae, while the more colourful shelducks use their flattened bright red beaks to sift through the mud for tiny molluscs.

The grey heron is a very patient bird which can wait motionless for long periods, watching for just the right moment to strike at its prey. As the tide falls, herons wade out into the shallow water of estuaries in search of eels and small flatfish.

GREY
HERON

AVOCET

CURLEW

TURNSTONE

OYSTERCATCHER

Summer

Winter

KNOT

Winter

Summer

WADERS

Large flocks of waders are found on the mudflats in winter, all of them in search of food. Although they all have fairly long legs and bills, each species is slightly different, so they do not compete with each other for the same food. The long legs and up-turned bill of the avocet are ideal for sweeping over soft mud in search of tiny shrimps, while the strong bill of the oystercatcher is more suited to pecking open tough shells like mussels. The long, down-curved bill of the curlew is helpful for reaching into the burrows of lugworms. The turnstone's short but strong bill can be used to flip over stones and shells, while the bills of the dunlin and knot can probe into soft mud for tiny molluscs and crustaceans.

Summer

Winter

DUNLIN

TRUE IDENTITY

The grey plover breeds in the far north of Europe, arriving in the south in late autumn. It can be recognized in flight by the black patches under the wings. Watch a flock of waders when they take off and look for these striking markings. In early spring the grey plover develops a back breast-patch as well.

117

Garden

Winter is an easy time for humans in the garden as there is not much work to do, but for the other creatures who live there life can still be a struggle since food can be much harder to find. For the wildlife watcher, there can be some exciting things to see from the windows of a house overlooking a garden.

HIBERNATING BAT

BROWN RAT

SLEEPY BATS

There are very few insects to be found in winter, so bats do not risk wasting energy by flying around searching for them. Instead, they find a secure place to hibernate and remain there until the spring. Several bats may use the same place, squeezing into tiny gaps under tiles on houses, or in hollow trees. Their body temperature falls and they breathe very slowly, unaware of the bad weather outside.

NOCTURNAL RATS

Black and brown rats are found in towns and gardens, although, being nocturnal, they may not be noticed. Both leave signs in the form of droppings and trails and, if they are common, their feeding signs will soon be noticed. Brown rats can become very bold, and feed in the open during the day if left undisturbed. Both species can transmit diseases to humans by contaminating water supplies. Rats can breed in winter if they have shelter in buildings or sewers, and produce about seven young in each litter.

BLACK RAT

118

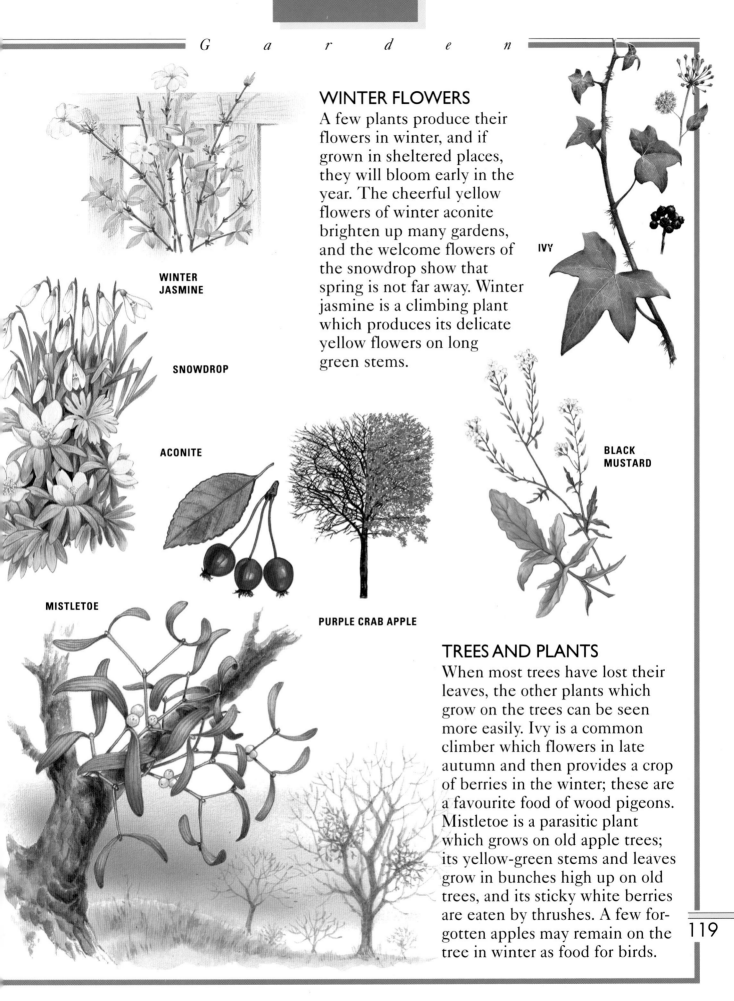

WINTER JASMINE

WINTER FLOWERS

A few plants produce their flowers in winter, and if grown in sheltered places, they will bloom early in the year. The cheerful yellow flowers of winter aconite brighten up many gardens, and the welcome flowers of the snowdrop show that spring is not far away. Winter jasmine is a climbing plant which produces its delicate yellow flowers on long green stems.

IVY

SNOWDROP

ACONITE

BLACK MUSTARD

MISTLETOE

PURPLE CRAB APPLE

TREES AND PLANTS

When most trees have lost their leaves, the other plants which grow on the trees can be seen more easily. Ivy is a common climber which flowers in late autumn and then provides a crop of berries in the winter; these are a favourite food of wood pigeons. Mistletoe is a parasitic plant which grows on old apple trees; its yellow-green stems and leaves grow in bunches high up on old trees, and its sticky white berries are eaten by thrushes. A few forgotten apples may remain on the tree in winter as food for birds.

119

TAWNY OWL

OWL ALERT

The tawny owl is quite at home in large gardens and parks, and its mournful call may be heard on winter nights. If you do hear it, it may be possible to get close enough to glimpse this owl in flight, but approach carefully as it is easily disturbed. If a roosting tree is located, look beneath it for pellets. These are the indigestible remains of its prey, and contain the bones, teeth and fur of small mammals.

GARDEN BIRDS

Many birds use gardens in winter, especially where food is provided for them. Some are resident birds like the robin and blue tit which inhabit the garden all year round, but others will be exciting visitors like the waxwing which will have migrated from the far north of Europe to escape a harsh winter, and will feed on the feast of berries found on ornamental trees and shrubs. If the garden is a peaceful place with very little to disturb them, the birds will become very confident and can then be observed closely.

OWL PELLETS

Look out for the tufted crest on the head of the waxwing, and its striking black facial markings, and the distinctive beautiful blue and yellow of the blue tit.

BLUE TIT

WAXWING

NESTBOX

Winter is a good time to build nestboxes and place them in the garden. Use wood strong enough to last out of doors, and make the box at least 12cm deep inside. Make the hole, which should measure 3cm across, about 20cm from the bottom of the box. Place the box where it will be out of the summer sun and safe from cats and troublesome humans!

Winter

Summer

STARLING

♀ **GREENFINCH**

DUNNOCK

FAVOURITE GARDEN BIRDS

The robin is a special favourite among garden bird-lovers. It can become very confident, and will follow a gardener around, often perching on a fork or wheel-barrow to watch for worms or insects. The dunnock is less often seen because of its streaked grey-brown plumage and retiring habits. The greenfinch is more colourful and more likely to be spotted as it visits seed-holders in search of food. The starling is a more noisy bird, usually present in large flocks.

ROBIN

Large gardens with big lawns and mature trees will attract the green woodpecker. It often feeds on the ground, using its long tongue to catch insects, but if disturbed will fly to a tree, perching behind the trunk, and peeping round to see if all is clear.

juv

♂

GREEN WOODPECKER

Glossary

Amphibian: An animal, such as a toad, which can live on land and water. Amphibians have no scales, but have moist skin.

Antlers: The horns of the male deer, grown each year and then cast off.

Beaver Lodge: The large home of a beaver built of sticks and mud, with an underwater entrance.

Berry: A juicy fruit, containing seeds, such as a currant.

Blossom: The flowers of a tree.

Bud: A small structure on a plant stem, containing young leaves or flowers. It usually remains closed up in winter.

Camouflage: Colourings which help a young animal blend with its surroundings.

Canopy: The topmost layer of branches and leaves in a wood.

Caterpillar: One stage in the life cycle of a butterfly or moth. The caterpillar hatches from an egg and feeds on plants before turning into a chrysallis.

Catkin: The male flower of a tree such as hazel, which produces pollen.

Chrysallis: The stage in the life cycle of a butterfly or moth which enables the caterpillar to develop into an adult. It looks still on the outside, but inside it is changing.

Climate: The long-term weather conditions of an area.

Cocoon: A protective covering for eggs, larvae or pupa.

Conifer: A tree which produces its seeds in cones.

Coniferous woodland: A woodland composed mainly of cone-bearing trees such as spruce or larch.

Courtship: The behaviour of animals before mating, when one tries to attract the interest of another.

Crown: The top part of a large tree, made up of branches, leaves and twigs.

Crustacean: An animal with jointed legs and a hard outer skin, such as a crab or a woodlouse.

Deciduous woodland: A wood comprised of trees which lose their leaves in winter.

Dormant: Sleeping for a prolonged period, such as a dormouse or bat in winter.

Estuary: The last stretch of a river where it meets the sea and the fresh water mixes with salt water.

Evergreen tree: A tree which keeps green leaves throughout the year, such as a holly or Scot's pine.

Flock: A large group of birds, or sometimes sheep.

Food chain: A sequence of organisms, starting with a plant, which are eaten by the next organism in the chain, transfering energy from one creature to the next, e.g., grass - rabbit - fox.

Food plant: A plant which is important as food to a particular species.

Fungi: Plants which feed on other plants, animals or dead living things, and do not require light.

Germination: The process by which seeds start to produce roots and shoots.

Hibernation: A long period of sleep during the winter, usually as a way of surviving harsh conditions when food is scarce.

Larva: The immature stage of an organism such as an insect, which may not resemble the adult in any way.

Leaf canopy: See Canopy.

Lichen: A complex plant made up of a fungus and an alga. Highly sensitive to pollution.

Life-cycle: The series of changes in the life of an organism from birth to death.

Mammal: A warm-blooded animal with a backbone. Mammals have hairy bodies, produce live young, and females feed them on milk.

Migrant: An animal which makes long journeys in search of food, or to escape harsh weather.

Migration: A long journey undertaken for some purpose, usually along a regular route.

Mole hill: A pile of earth thrown up by the burrowing activities of a mole.

Mollusc: A soft-bodied creature protected by a shell which may be in one or two parts. Some molluscs, such as slugs, have lost their shells.

Nectar: A sugary liquid produced by flowers to attract insects.

Nocturnal: Active at night, like an owl or bat.

Nymph: The immature stage of an insect, such as a damselfly.

Ovipostor: The pointed structure used by an insect such as a bush-cricket to deposit eggs inside a plant.

Parasite: A plant or animal which lives on or in the body of another living thing and obtains all its food from it.

Pesticide: A poisonous substance used to kill plants or animals which may be pests to farmers or gardeners.

Pollard: To remove the head or crown of a tree but leave the trunk growing.

Pollen: The male reproductive cells of a plant, produced inside the flower, and carried to another flower to fertilise the female cells by insects or the wind.

Pollination: The process in which pollen is carried from flower to flower to fertilise the female cells.

Pollution: Harming the environment with poisons.

Predator: An animal which catches other animals for its food.

Pupa: See chrysallis.

Reptile: A cold-blooded animal with a backbone and scaly skin.

Rodent: A small mammal with chisel-like front teeth for gnawing its food.

Roosting: The resting and sleeping behaviour of birds.

Rut: The time of courtship of deer and wild goats and sheep.

Scavenger: An animal which feeds on dead plant and animal material.

Seed: The first stage in the life of a flowering plant, containing an embryo and a supply of food.

Sett: The underground home of a badger.

Spawning: The process of egg-laying in fish and amphibians.

Spore: The first stage in the life-cycle of a fungus, or of simple plants like mosses and ferns.

Strand line: The highest point reached by the tide on a beach where seaweeds, shells and other debris are cast ashore.

Territory: The area defended by an animal in which it makes its home.

Toadstool: The part of a fungus which lives above the ground and is responsible for producing spores.

Acknowledgements

t = top, b = bottom, c = centre, r = right, l = left, u = upper, cll = centre lower left, clr = centre lower right, cul = centre upper left, cur = centre upper right, p = panel

ILLUSTRATIONS

Fred Anderson, Bernard Thornton Artists: 10 (p), 18 (p), 22 (p), 48 (p), 92 (p, 114 (p)

Priscilla Barrett: 27 (bl), 59 (bl), 65 (tl), 96 (cr, br)

A Beckett, Garden Studios: 80 (p), 84 (cl, cr, br), 88 (p), 102 (p)

John Bignall, Linden Artists: 50 (cul, cll), (cur, clr), 52 (tr), 53 (tl), 96 (p)

Isabel Bowring, The Gallery: 13 (tl, tr, bl), 15 (tr), 21 (tl, cl), 28, 33 (cur, clr), 36 (b), 43, 68 (tl, cul, cll, bl), 81 (tr), 88

Peter Bull: 94 (b)

Jim Channell: 26 (p), 39 (box), 49 (tr), 54 (p), 65 (bl), 112 (br)

Roger Gorridge, Garden Studios: 12 (tr, c, br, bl), 14, 20 (tl, cl, cr, cl, br), 23 (bl), 26 (cr), 32 (cl, cr, b), 33 (tl, cul, cll, bl), 38 (br), 40 (br), 41 (bl, br), 46 (br), 47, 49 (bc), 62 (br), 66 (tr), 67 (br), 69 (cur), 77 (tl, cr), 83 (tl), 95 (c), 111 (br), 114 (tr), 119 (cu, cl, cr)

Miranda Grey, Ian Flemming Associates: 68 (br), 69 (cur)

Alma Hathway, Bernard Thornton Artists: 53 (tr), 97, 115 (c, br)

Steve Holden, Garden Studios: 44 (p)

David Holmes: 39 (tr), 108 (t)

Gillian Kenny, Linden Artists: 49 (cr), 53 (b)

Roger Kent: 42 (cul, tr), 46 (bc), 49 (cr), 58 (bc), 62 (tl, cur), 67 (tl), 69 (cr), bcr), 83 (br), 102 (tl), 104 (tl, cul), 104 (bl, cr), 107

Ian Lewington: 11 (r), 16 (tr, tl), 19 (tl, tr, cr), 27 (cb), 34 (tr, cr), 37 (tl, tr), 45 (clr, cll, clr, br), 48 (b), 64 (cl, bl, tr, cr), 70 (tl, cul), 74 (br), 75 (ul, cul, b), 81 (cr, br), 86, 90 (bl), 106 (tl), 106 (cr), 110 (cl, bl), 120 (ur, c), 121 (tl, cul)

Stephen Lings, Linden Artists: 17 (l), 24 (tr), 25 (tr), 27 (tr), 34 (tl), 41 (tr), 45 (tl), 51 (tl), 56 (c, bl, br), 64 (tl), 75 (clr), 94 (cu), 99 (ul), 110 (tl), 115 (t), 116 (b), 117 (cul), 117 (bl), 120 (b)

Mick Loates: 29 (t, cl, ccl, ccr, cr, br), 54 (tl, cl), 55 (tl, cur, clr, b), 62 (clr)

Alan Male, Linden Artists: 23 (tl), 33 (tr), 36 (t), 42 (b), 44, 46 (tl, cl), 57, 60 (tr), 63 (cr, bl, bm, br), 69 (cul), 74 (tl, c), 92 (br), 93 (tr, cul, cur, clr)

Doreen McGuinness: 18, 27 (br), 34 (b), 35 (tr, cul, cll), 42 (cr), 50 (tl), 59 (t, box, br), 65 (bl), 72, 73 (c), 82 (tl, tc), 96 (tl), 102 (b), 103 (cr, b), 108 (b), 109 (tl), 110 (p), 112 (tr, cl), 113, 118

David More: 10, 11 (box), 14 (p), 17 (tl, cl, bl), 19 (cl, bl), 22 (bl), 26 (cl, bl), 32 (tr), 36 (p), 37 (cl, cr, b), 58 (tl), 64 (p), 66 (cul, cll, bl, br), 68 (p), 70 (b), 71, 72 (p), 76, 80, 81 (tl, cl), 85 (br), 87 (cl), 91, 93 (bl, bc, br), 105, 106 (b, p), 111 (tl, tr), 119 (tl, cl, bl)

Robert Morton, Bernard Thornton Artists: 23 (br), 39 (tl), 68 (cb), 82 (tr), 103 (tl, tr), 109 (tr)

Tricia Newell, John Martin Artists: 20 (tr), 21 (bl, tr), 36 (c), 46 (tr), 69 (tl), 69 (cll, bl), 73 (tl), 87 (cr, br), 92 (tr)

Jane Pickering: 24 (tl, cl, c, cb, cr), 25 (bl), 26 (c), 42 (tl), 52, 58 (box, bl, cr, br), 62 (bl, bc), 82 (bl, bc, br), 83 (bl, bc), 84 (tr, bl), 85 (cl), 85 (tr), 89 (tl, br), 99 (b), 104 (cll), 104 (br), 114 (b)

Chris Shields, Linden Artists: 13 (br), 21 (br), 73 (b), 87 (tl)

Catharine Slade, Ian Fleming Associates: 42 (cur), 104 (tr)

Phil Weare, Linden Artists: 8-9, 15 (tl), 15 (bl), 23 (tr), 29 (bl), 30-31, 32 (p), 40 (p), 50 (bl, br), 51 (cll, br), 54 (b), 55 (tr), 60 (tl, cl, b, p), 61, 63 (tl, box), 78-79, 84 (p), 100-101

David Webb, Linden Artists: 51 (tr, cul), 69 (tr)

Ian Willis: 11 (tr, cr, br, tl, cl), 16 (cr, b), 19 (br), 25 (cl), 27 (ct), 41 (tl, tc, cul, cr), 45 (cul, ctr), 45 (bl, bc), 48 (tr, cr), 48 (tl, tc), 49 (cl), 56 (t), 70 (cl), 74 (clr), 75 (cl, cr), 81 (bl), 90 (tl, cul, cur, cll), 94 (tl), 94 (tr), 99 (tc, tr, cr, lc), 102 (cl, cr), 106 (tc, tr), 110 (br), 116 (t, cl), 117 (tl, tc, tr), 117 (cll), 121 (cll, cr, br)

Roy Wiltshire, 2-D: 35 (br)

PHOTOGRAPHS

Heather Angel/Biofotos: 99; Bruce Coleman: Nigel Blake 49; Jane Burton 29; Adrian Davies 23; Martin Dohrn 46; Dennis Green 33; Jan van de Kam 16 (br); Gordon Langsbury 7, 116; George McCarthy 43; Francisco Marquez 56; Flip de Nooyer 77; Hans Reinhard 13,47, 66 (tl) Kim Taylor 101; Michael Viard 10; Konrad Wothe 121; Eric Crichton: 71; NHPA: Laurie Campbell 12, 80; Stephen Dalton 26, 28, 31, 65 (tr), 69, 95, 120 (br); Manfred Danegger 34; Martin Garwood 91 (tr); JS Gifford 58; EA Janes 48, 54(bl), 65 (bl), 90; Michael Leech 75; Natural Image: Robert Dickson 45; David Element 24; Robin Fletcher 38; Bob Gibbons 14, 67; Peter Wilson 109; Nature Photographers: SC Bisserot 72, 36; Frank V Blackburn 16 (tl), 106; K Blamire 9; Nicholas Brown 57; Brinsley Burbidge 91; Robin Bush 63; NA Callow 74 (r); Kevin Carlson 114, 115 (bl); C Carver 86; Hugh Clark 120 (tl); AJ Cleave 25; Ron Croucher 21; John Doe 83; CH Gomershall 15; EA Janes 6 (tl, tr, bl, br); 105; Hugh Miles 113; Owen Newman 27; Charles Palmar 115 (tr); Paul Sterry 20, 37, 54 (tr), 60, 73(t,) 73(b), 79, 87, 89, 92, 97, 111; Roger Tidman 66 (br), 117; Neil Wilmore 55; Alan R Outen: 85

Index

Figures in bold indicate illustrations.

acacia, false 93, 93
aconite, winter 119
adder 9, 44, 44
alder 13, 26, 26, 86
alder buckthorn 26, 26
alpine snowbell 111, 111
anemone
    beadlet 31, 30, 52,
    parasitic 53
    sea 53
    wood 12
ant, wood 36, 36, 70
aphid 68
    woolly 20
apple 76, 76, 119
    purple crab 119,
    119
    wild crab 19, 19
ash 10, 10, 105, 105
    manna 105
aspen 17, 17
autumn 79-99
avocet 117, 117

badger 35, 35, 79, 79
balm of Gilead 93, 93
bat 9, 28, 35, 72, 72, 79,
    118, 118
    leisler's 35
    pipistrelle 72, 72
    serotine 35
beaver 27, 27
beech 80, 80, 105, 105
bee 9, 9, 10, 12, 13, 19,
    20, 23, 32, 38, 40,
    67, 95
    buff-tailed
    bumble 69
    bumble 95
    honey 92, 92, 95
    white-tailed
    bumble 92, 92
beetle 28, 85
    cockchafer 69
    devil's coach-
    horse 93, 93
    great diving 61,
    61
    great silver 61,
    oil 23, 23

beetle
    whirlygig 60
bilberry 38, 38
bindweed, field 77, 77
binoculars 5
birch 86
    downy 17, 17
bird-watching 5, 7, 101,
    120-121
bittern 56, 56
blackberry, wild 32, 32
blackbird 6, 6, 90, 90
blackthorn 66, 66
bluebell 12
bracken 47, 47
brambling 78, 78
breeding 7, 9, 22, 35, 48,
    62, 73, 99
broomrape, common 41
buckler fern 38, 38
buckthorn 10, 10, 13
bugle 20
bull 65, 65
bullfinch 81, 81
bullhead 54, 54
burdock 101
buttercup, meadow 40,
    40
butterfly 9, 12, 13, 20,
    23, 32, 40, 43, 49,
    62, 68, 81, 88
    blue 43
    brimstone 13, 13
    chalkhill blue 43
    clouded yellow 23
    common blue 43
    dingy skipper 43
    gatekeeper 88, 88
    grizzled skipper
    43
    holly blue 43, 88,
    88
    large skipper 43,
    43
    large white 68, 68
    orange tip 13, 13
    painted lady 88,
    88
    peacock 9, 9, 88,
    88
    purple emperor
    33, 33
    purple hairstreak
    13

    red admiral 81, 81
    red underwing 13,
    13
    scotch argus 21,
    21
    silver-studded
    blue 43
    silver-Y 23
    small blue 43
    small copper 43,
    43
    small skipper 43,
    43
    small tortoiseshell
    68, 68, 88
    small white 68
    speckled wood 4,
    4, 33, 33
    swallowtail 15
    wood white 36, 36
    yellow brimstone
    101

caddis fly 9, 9, 28, 28, 55
camouflage 15, 16, 21,
    25, 29, 31, 34, 45,
    48, 50, 51, 88
carp 29
caterpillar 13, 15, 20, 21,
    68, 81, 85, 87
    garden tiger moth
    73, 73
    swallowtail 15, 15
catkins 10, 11, 11
cat 72, 72, 73, 100
cedar 91, 91
chaffinch 37, 37
chamois 112, 112
cherry 105
    sour 71, 71
    weeping Japanese
    70
chestnut
    horse 71, 71, 105
    sweet 105
chickweed
    common 77, 77
    wintergreen 38,
    38
clover, white 67, 67
cockle 24, 24
cockroach 73, 73
collecting 5, 105

coltsfoot 95, 95, 77
conduct 7, 48
cones 36, 37, 84, 85, 85,
    86, 107, 107
conservation 7
coot 56, 56
coppicing 20
corn bunting 41, 41
cornflower 67, 67
courtship 9, 27, 48
cow parsley 8, 8, 20
crab 50
    hermit 30, 30, 51,
    51, 53
    masked 51, 51
    shore 50, 50
    spiny spider 50,
    50
cranesbill 40
crayfish, freshwater 54,
    54
cricket
    bog bush 46, 46
    house 93, 93
    mole- 42, 42
    wood 81, 81
crocus 69
crossbill 86, 86
crow, carrion 64, 64
cuckoo 19, 19
    flower 23
curlew 45, 45, 117, 117
cyclops 55, 55
cypress
    Leyland 91
    swamp 17, 17

daffodil, wild 59
daisy 77, 83, 83
    ox-eye 67, 67
damselfly
    banded
    demoiselle 57, 57
    blue-tailed 63
    large red 63
dandelion 77, 77
dead-nettle, red and
    white 95, 95
deer 9, 102, 105
    fallow 39, 39, 79
    muntjac 82, 82
    red 112, 112
    roe 103, 103

sika 103, 103
dove
    collared 94
    rock 31
dragonfly
    common hawker
    63, 63
    emperor 63, 63
duck, eider 48, 48
duckweed 62, 62
dunlin 117, 117
dunnock 121, 121

eagle, golden 110, 110
earthworm 35, 41, 79
earwig 73, 73
eel 29, 29
egg laying 9, 13, 15, 20,
    24, 27, 28, 29, 46,
    63, 63, 68, 69, 74,
    87
elder 80
elm, wych 66, 66
equipment 5, 5
estuaries 114-117

farmland 64-67
fieldfare 90, 90
finches 81, 86
flocks, feeding 86, 102
flote grass 26, 26
flounder 51, 51
flowers 9, 9, 10, 13, 19,
    20
    wild 10, 12, 13,
    31, 67
fly 33
    drone 74, 74
    fruit 85
    house 74, 74
    hover 32, 33, 33
    kelp fly 97
    sawflies 36, 36,
    37
flycatchers
    pied 34, 34
    spotted 70
food chain 29
fox 9, 35, 45, 100, 100
    arctic 109, 109
    red 34, 34
foxglove 33, 33
frog 9, 63, 69,
    common 62, 62
frogbit 14, 14
froghopper, common 69,
    69

fulmar 49, 49
fungi 6, 83, 84, 85, 88,
    89, 104
    artist's 104
    birch polypore
    83, 83
    blushing bracket
    104, 104
    bracket 6, 6, 104
    brown roll-rim 83
    candle snuff 89,
    89
    cauliflower 84, 84
    cup 104
    ear pick 107, 107
    fairy ring
    champignon 89,
    89
    false chanterelle
    84, 84
    field mushroom
    42
    fly agaric 79, 79,
    83
    giant puffball 82,
    83
    hairy leather-
    bracket 104, 104
    honey 84
    herald of the
    winter 107, 107
    jelly antler 85, 85,
    107, 107
    meadow coral 42,
    85, 85
    orange peel 89, 89
    penny bun 84
    plums and custard
    84, 84
    scaly wood 83
    scarlet elf-cup 104
    shady ink-caps
    42, 42
    shaggy parasol 42,
    42
    slipper jack 84
    spindle shank 82
    stinkhorn,
    common 82
    velvet shank 104,
    104
    violet conifer
    bracket 107, 107
    wood warts 104,
    104
    yellow-milk cup
    104
fungus gnats 85

gannet 49, 49
gardens 118-121
garlic, wild 12, 12
ginkgo 70
goldcrest 106, 106
golden
    oriole 11
    plover 45
    rod 79
goldfinch 19, 95
goldfish 62, 62
goose
    Canada 62, 62
    Brent 116
gorse 45, 46, 46
goshawk 106, 106
grasses 40
grasshopper
    common green 42,
    42
    meadow 42, 42
    mottled 42
    stripe-winged 42
great mullein 77, 77
grebe, great crested 27,
    27
greenfinch 121, 121
greenfly 92
greenshank 17, 17
groundsel 95, 95
grouse, red 45, 45
guillemot 49, 49
gull 25, 116
    black-headed 25
    common 116, 116
    great black-
    headed 99, 99
    herring 31, 99, 99,
    116
    lesser black-
    backed 99, 99

hand lenses 5
hare 65, 65
    mountain 110,
    113, 113
harrier 45
hawfinch 78, 78, 81, 81
hawthorn 8, 8
hazel 19, 19
heath and moor 44-47
heath speedwell 38, 38
heather 38
    bell 47, 47
hedgehog 9, 101, 102,
    103, 103
heron, grey 116, 116

hibernation 9, 10, 21, 24,
    35, 79, 84, 88, 92, 101,
    102, 103, 118
hide, making a 7, 7
holly 101, 101, 105, 105
hornbeam 105
house martin 94, 94

Indian bean tree 70
insects 8, 12, 22, 23, 36,
    40, 41, 46, 54, 57,
    60, 63, 95, 96,
    102, 106, 107
iris, yellow flag 58, 58
ivy 95, 119, 119
    ground 77

jackdaw 74, 74
jasmine, winter 119, 119
jay 70, 70
jellyfish 51, 51
juniper 37, 37

kestrel 75, 75
kingfisher 56, 56, 58
kite, black 64, 64
kittiwake 116
knot 117, 117

laburnam 71, 71
lacewing, green 92, 92
ladybird 68, 68
lakes 26-29
lapwing 41, 41
larch 37, 37
leafhopper, red and
    black 21, 21
leech 55, 55
lichen 53, 110, 112
    mountain 111,
    111
limpet
    common 52, 52
    river 54, 54
linnet 45, 45
lizard 9
    common 44, 44
    sand 44, 44
loosestrife
    purple 62, 62
    yellow 58, 58
lords and ladies 33, 33
lynx 113, 113

magpie 75, 75
mallard 27, 27
maple 105
    field 66, 66
    smooth Japanese 70
marmot, alpine 113, 113
marram grass 31, 98, 98
marsh marigold 14
marshes 14-17, 49
mayfly 55, 57, 57
meadow cranesbill 41
meadow pipit 41, 41
meadows 40-43
migration 23, 34, 94, 120
milk parsley 15, 15
millipede 85
mink, European 59, 59
minnow 55, 55
mistletoe 6, 119, 119
mole 18, 18
molluscs 24, 52, 54
moorhen 90, 90
mosquito 57, 57, 60, 60
mosses 38
moth 40
    death's head hawk 23, 23
    emperor 46, 46
    garden tiger 73
    lappet moth 21, 21
    larvae 36
    pine beauty 85, 85
    pine hawk 87, 87
    tiger 72
mouflon 112, 112
moulding 76, 76
moulting 9
mountains 110-113
mouse 35, 64, 82
    dormice 9, 19, 82
    hazel 82
    house 72, 73, 73, 100, 100
    wood 35, 35
    yellow-necked 82, 82
mussel 24, 52, 117

necklace shell 99, 99
nectar 13, 20
nestboxes 120
nesting 9, 16, 18, 27, 35, 36, 45, 48, 56, 65, 73, 86
    sites 11, 19, 26, 30, 31, 40, 41, 45, 91
netting 54
nettle, stinging 68, 77, 81
newt 9, 28, 63
    palmate 63, 63
night creatures 35
nightingale 11, 11
nightjar 45, 45
note taking 4, 5
nuthatch 34, 34

oak 10, 10, 80, 81, 105, 105
octopus 50, 50
orchid 40, 40
    bee 40, 40
    common spotted 67, 67
    greater butterfly 40, 40
    purple 40, 40
    pyramidal 40, 40
osier 58, 58
otter 59, 59
owl
    barn 64, 64
    little 64, 64
    long-eared 106, 106
    tawny 101, 120, 120
oystercatcher 24, 117, 117

pansy, wild 49, 49
parks and gardens 68-71, 88-91
partridge 19
    grey 19
    red-legged 19
pear tree 76, 76
peppery furrow shell 114, 114
periwinkle 52
    edible 52
    flat 52
pesticides 40, 67, 68
pets 72
pheasant 64, 64
photography 4, 4, 6, 6
pigeon 31
    feral 75, 75
    wood 102, 102
pike 55
pine marten 108, 108
pine, mountain 111, 111

plane, London 76, 76
plover
    golden 45, 45
    grey 117
    ringed 25, 25
plum tree, purple-leaved 76, 76
polecat 39, 39
pollen 10, 11, 13, 20, 33, 92
pollination 32
pollution 7, 7, 55, 59, 76
pond skater 60, 60
ponds 60-63
pondweed, Canadian 62, 62
poplar 11
    Lombardy 93, 93
    white 10, 10
poppy 66, 66
prawn 51
predators 24, 35, 45, 62, 88, 113
prickly saltwort 114, 114
primrose 8, 8, 13, 20
ptarmigan 110, 110
puffin 31, 48, 48
purple moor grass 47, 47

rabbit 12, 42, 42
ragwort 95, 95
raspberry, wild 32, 32
rat, black and brown 118, 118
raven 110, 110
razor shell 24, 24
razorbill 31
redpoll 86, 86
redshank 16, 16
redstart 34, 34, 74, 74
redwing 90, 90
reedmace 58, 58
reeds 26, 26
reindeer 109, 109
reptiles 44
rivers 54-59
roach 29
robin 120, 121, 121
rock pipit 99, 99
rock pools 31, 31, 52, 53
rock sea spurrey 31
rook 64, 64
rose
    dog 33, 33
    guelder 76, 76
rosebay willowherb 77, 77
rowan 87

rudd 29
rush, flowering 14, 14

sage, wood 38, 38
salmon 115, 115
sandhopper 51, 97, 96
scarlet pimpernel 67, 67
Scots pine 85, 85
scurvy-grass, common 22, 22
sea
    bindweed 98, 98
    buckthorn 22, 22
    campion 22, 22
    holly 31, 49
    kale 98, 98
    lavender 49, 49
    lemon 9, 24, 24
    lettuce 53
    orange 51, 51
    rocket 98, 98
    sandwort 98
    slater 96, 97, 97
seal
    common 30, 30, 50, 50, 96, 96
    grey 96, 96
    monk 96, 96
seashores 9, 22-25, 30-31, 48-53
seaweed 9, 53, 96, 97, 99
    furbelow 97
    sea bootlace 97
    sea kelp 97, 97
    sea oak or pondweed 97
    knotted or egg wrack 53
    oarweed 97, 97
    serrated wrack 53
    spiral or flat wrack 53
shag 48, 48
sheep 47
sheep's fescue 47, 47
shelduck 116
shellfish 50
shepherd's purse 95, 95
shieldbug, hawthorn 21, 21
shrew 65, 97
    common 65, 65
    lesser white-toothed 96
    pygmy 96, 96
    water 26, 26, 27
shrike, great grey 45, 45
shrimp 31, 50, 117

silver fir, common 111
siskin 86, 86
sketching 4, 4
skua 116
    arctic 116
    great 116
skylark 41, 41
sloes, 66, 66
slug 35, 41, 85, 107
snail 85
    garden 93, 93, 101
    great pond 61, 61, 62
    ramshorn 29, 29
snake
    grass 69, 69
    smooth 44, 44
snipe 16, 16
snow bunting 110, 110
snowdrop 119, 119
song, birds 10, 11, 16, 19, 34, 41
sparrow, house, 75, 75
sparrowhawk 102, 102
spawning 44, 62, 63
spider
    garden 93, 93
    orb-web 46, 46
spindle 80, 81
spores 82, 89
spring 8-29
spruce
    Norway 106, 106
    sitka 37, 37
squid 50, 50
squirrel 79, 80
    European 108
    grey 103, 103
    red 108, 108
starfish 52, 52
    brittle-star, common 52, 52
    burrowing 52
    cushion 52
    spiny 52, 52
    star cushion 52
    sun-star, common 52
starling 101, 121, 121
stick insect, water 15, 15
stickleback, three-spined 54, 54
stinking hellebore 102, 102
stitchwort 8, 8
    greater 12
stoat 8, 8, 18, 18

stonechat 45
stonefly 57, 57
storksbill, common 114, 114
strand line 96-99
strawberry, wild 32, 32
summer 30-77
sundew 46, 46, 47
swallow 41, 41
swan 27, 27
swift 74, 75
sycamore 32, 32

tadpole 61, 62, 63
teasel 101
tench 29
tern, Arctic 31, 49, 49
territories 11, 25, 33, 35, 39, 41, 63, 86
thrift 31, 49, 49
thrush 90
    mistle 90, 90
    song 70
tit
    blue 120, 120
    coal 37, 37
    crested 86, 86
    great 11
toadflax 67, 67
toad 9, 62, 63
    natterjack 44, 44
    tormentil 38, 38
towns 72-77, 92-95
tracks, making casts of 39
tree of heaven 105
tree spotting 105
treecreeper 81, 81
trees 26, 70, 79, 91
trout, brown 55, 55
tufted vetch 38
turnstone 117, 117

urchin, heart 30, 30

violet, common dog 20, 20
vole 64, 65, 65
    bank 65
    field 65
    water 59, 59

waders 25, 116, 117
wagtail 56
    grey 56, 56

    pied 94
    yellow 56, 56
walnut 105
warbler 19
    cetti's 16
    Dartford 45, 45
    sedge 16, 16
wasp 40, 69, 69, 87, 95, 95
    ichneumon 87, 87
    wood 87, 87
water
    boatmen 61, 61
    crowfoot 58, 58
    louse 55, 55
    scorpion 60, 60
water-lily 14, 14
    white 14
waxwing 120, 120
weasel 35
whelk 24, 25, 51
    common 52
    thick-lipped dog 24, 52
wild service tree 80, 80
wildcat 113, 113
willow 17, 58
    crack 58, 58
    pussy 17
    weeping 66, 66
winkle 24, 24
winter 100-121
wood sorrel 12
woodcock 11
woodland
    coniferous 36-39, 84-87, 106-109
    deciduous 10, 32-35, 80-83, 102-105
woodpecker 10
    great spotted 11
    green 121, 121
    lesser spotted 11
worm 50, 115
    lugworm 115, 115, 117
    ragworm 115
wren 106, 106

yellow archangel 33, 33
yellowhammer 41, 41
yew 76, 76
Yorkshire fog 47, 46